About the author

A full-time writer and journalist, Graeme Donald's broadcasting experience includes setting the questions for *Back to Square One*, a quiz programme broadcast on Radio 2, Radio 4 and the World Service, and soon to be televised. He has written a column expounding his knowledge of etymology in *Today* newspaper for the last seven years, and published two books based on the column, *Things You Didn't Know You Didn't Know* and *More Things You Didn't Know You Didn't Know*. He has also published *The Dictionary of Modern Phrase*.

The Pocket Book of Pub Quizzes

Two thousand tantalising questions with intriguing answers . . .

SUE AND GRAEME DONALD

LONDON · SYDNEY · NEW YORK · TOKYO · SINGAPORE · TORONTO

First published in Great Britain by Pocket Books, 1995
An imprint of Simon & Schuster Ltd
A Paramount Communications Company

Simon & Schuster Ltd
West Garden Place
Kendal Street
London W2 2AQ

Simon & Schuster of Australia Pty Ltd
Sydney

A CIP catalogue record for this book is available from the British Library

ISBN 0-671-85350-3

Typeset in Footlight and Gill Sans 11/13pt by
Palimpsest Book Production Limited, Polmont, Stirlingshire
Printed and bound in Great Britain by
HarperCollins Manufacturing, Glasgow

CONTENTS

Section 1: Questions

Section 2: Answers

ENTERTAINMENT AND THE ARTS

1. What is the name connection between Ma Larkin in recent television adaptations of *The Darling Buds of May* and Bob in *The Likely Lads*?
2. In the run-up to the 1953 Coronation, how many television sets were sold? (Allow within 25,000 either way.)
3. Who was the question-master of *Round Britain Quiz* and the *Brains Trust* and a panellist on *What's My Line?*
4. Which popular children's programme ran for only twenty-six episodes but was repeated frequently between 1953 and 1970?
5. Peter Hawkins was the voice behind Bill and Ben, the Flowerpot Men, he later went on to provide the voices for which evil characters in *Dr Who?*

6. In 1953, Michael Crawford and David Hemmings appeared in a school series, what was the name of the series and what was the name of the school?

7. By what name was Richard Hearn better known?

8. Which programme has been compered by Michael Aspel, David Jacobs, Judith Chalmers, Terry Wogan and Angela Rippon?

9. What artistic connection is shared by Len Deighton, Graeme Sutherland, Man Ray and Mabel Lucie Atwell?

10. What occupation did Jean Alexander, Mao Tse-Tung, and Philip Larkin have in common?

11. Which novel was made into a film twice – the first starred Michael Redgrave and Donald Pleasance and the second John Hurt and Richard Burton?

12. What do these two films have in common: *The Hound of the Baskervilles* and *The Man who was Sherlock Holmes?*

13. Who played Vicomte de Valmont in Stephen Frears' film version of *Dangerous Liaisons*?

14. American actress Uma Thurman starred in *Dangerous Liaisons* and *Robin Hood.* What was the coincidence involved in the film versions of both these stories?

15. What recent surprise film hit starred Paul Mercurio?

16. Which 1978 series ran for 13 episodes and starred Julia Foster and John Stride as a husband and wife amateur detective partnership?

17. Which British writer wrote his plays in short-hand?

18. Who played opposite Twiggy as the Boy Friend?

19. Who played Trisha in the film version of *Educating Rita?*

20. Who wrote the Booker prize winner *Possession*?

21. Who is the author of *Chatterton*, *English Music* and *Hawksmoor*?

22. Who wrote *The History Man*?

23. Who is the quiz-master on Radio Four's *The News Quiz*?

24. Name Phil and Jill Archer's four children.

25. Still with the Archers, what is the name of the series' fictional village and county?

26. Which book starts with the words: 'It was a fine, sunny, showery day in April. The big studio window was open at the top, and let in a pleasant breeze from the north-west'.

27. Who is the author of *A Touch of Frost?* For an

extra point, who played Frost in the recent TV adaptation?

28. What is the name of the Radio Four programme that runs from 6.30 a.m. to 9 a.m. Monday to Saturday?

29. Which radio programme is currently (1994) presented by Jenni Murray?

30. In which year did *Coronation Street* begin?

31. Which television series of the sixties and seventies developed from *Police Surgeon* starring Ian Hendry?

32. Who played Dr Kildare?

33. How many episodes of *Fawlty Towers* were made?

34. What were the names of the characters that John Thaw and Dennis Waterman played in *The Sweeney*?

35. Of which programme did a TV company boss say: 'it was cruel and sexist and I don't think tipping custard over people made particularly exciting television'?

36. In what year did Salman Rushdie go into hiding?

37. Who played Sarah Connor in the *Terminator* films?

38. Who was Bridget Fonda's flatmate in *Single, White Female?*

39. Who had children called Suzanna, Hamnet and Judith?

40. Which couple had a son called Astralabe?

41. Which film opens with a scene of men running along a beach?

42. Which musician/composer wrote 'The Long March' and 'I'll Find My Way Home'?

43. What was the real name of the 'Singing Nun'?

44. Who wrote *A Kind of Loving*?

45. Who starred in the television play of *Shadowlands*?

46. What is the shortest sentence in the Bible?

47. Which Shakespearian lady said: 'all the perfumes of Arabia will not sweeten this little hand'?

48. In which book is Billy Casper the anti-hero?

49. In which book is Ann chased by Mr Loomis?

50. Who wrote *Rubyfruit Jungle?*

51. Who wrote *Zen and the Art of Motorcycle Maintenance?*

52. What was Christoph Gluck's middle name?

53. What was the title of the first Sherlock Holmes tale?

54. In the 1800s, who devised the first Christmas annual?

55. Who wrote *The Mandelbaum Gate* and *Girls of Slender Means*?

56. Which book by Andrea Newman was made into a television series starring Trevor Eve as a womanising author?

57. Which member of the Rock Follies cast went on to sing on the original recording of *Evita?*

58. Which famous couple were portrayed by Edward Fox and Cynthia Harris?

59. What was the name of the feminist magazine which ceased publication in 1992?

60. In *The Likely Lads*, what was Bob's girlfriend called?

61. The writers of *The Likely Lads* penned a 1970s BBC series starring Brian Wilde and a hugely successful comedy-drama for ITV in the 1980s. Name both series.

62. Who was the chairman of *Ask the Family*?

63. The Monty Python team assembled for the film *The Life of Brian*. Which former pop star owned

the company that made the film and had a one line part in a crowd scene?

64. Which play starring Alison Steadman was the first full-length television drama to be partly improvised?

65. In the 1970 film adaptation of *Wuthering Heights*, who played Heathcliff?

66. What detective did Nicholas Ball play?

67. How many programmes were made for the spoof police series *Police Squad*?

68. Which actor took the part of Salieri in the film of *Amadeus*?

69. George Archer Shee was a real life character whose story was subsequently dramatized by Terrence Rattigan. What was the play?

70. Which David Mamet play centres on a real estate office in Chicago?

71. Who wrote *Frankenstein – The Modern Prometheus?*

72. In the 1994 BAFTA awards, which film won the Lloyds Bank customers' choice for best film?

73. Film critic Kim Newman said of a 1989 hit film: 'it proves that a female director can make a film just as dreadful as any male hack director ...

we're talking horrible, horrible, horrible ...' What film is it?

74. At the end of *The Prisoner*, Patrick McGoohan unmasks Number One and finds what?

75. Peg Entwhistle, a bit part actress, leapt to fame on September 18 1932. How?

76. Whose silent film star career was finished when he was charged with rape and murder?

77. What working style was common to the following writers: Lewis Carroll, Ernest Hemingway, Vladimir Nabokov and Virginia Woolf?

78. What is the name of Radio Four's long running satirical programme based on the week's news events?

79. What is the name of the artist who has preserved a shark in a tank of formaldehyde?

80. Which famous oratorio was first performed in the Fishamble Street Music Hall, Dublin in 1772? All proceeds intended to release debtors from the local debtors' prison.

81. Which composer wrote *Nixon in China*?

82. Which Belgian surrealist artist painted *Time Transfixed?*

83. How many 'Brandenburg Concertos' did Bach write?

84. The television programme *The New Statesman* has theme music originally composed by Mussorgsky. What is the name of the whole work?

85. Which British composer wrote 'The Banks of Green Willow'?

86. In what field of decorative arts did René Lalique rise to fame?

87. In which Shakespeare play does Owen Glendower (Owain Glyndwr) appear?

88. Who designed the Glasgow School of Art?

89. Which famous painting by Edvard Munch was stolen from a Norwegian art gallery and recovered in 1994?

90. Which designer and craftsman founded the Kelmscott Press?

91. By what collective name were William Holman-Hunt, Dante Gabriel Rossetti and John Everett Millais known?

92. What was designed by Sir Joseph Paxton and opened on May 1 1851?

93. What do Marlon Brando and Frank Sinatra have in common?

94. Who said: 'I do all my writing in bed; everyone knows I do all my best work there'?

95. Name two animals to make prints in the cement outside Mann's Chinese Theatre.

96. Which book opens with the following lines: 'I was born in Bombay . . . once upon a time. No, that won't do'?

97. Which artist/sculptor won the Turner Prize in 1993 with a concrete model of a house?

98. Who was the hostess who couldn't add up in *The Golden Shot*?

99. Which humorous travel writer has written *The Lost Continent* and *Here and There*?

100. Who broadcasts a *Letter From America?*

101. Which opera singer sang at Prince Charles's wedding?

102. Which band had an unusual and unexpected top ten hit in 1975 with 'Scotch on the Rocks'?

103. Which American singer/songwriter sang 'Wanderin', 'Fire and Rain' and 'Sweet Baby James'?

104. Carly Simon won an award for 'Let the River Run'. It was the theme music for which 1988 film?

105. Which dance did Byron object to, saying that it involved 'Lewd grasp and lawless contact'?

106. Which songwriter penned 'Oh, Susanna' and 'I Dream of Jeannie'?

107. Which actresses played Thelma and Louise?

108. In which BBC comedy series did actress Rachel Bell keep asking: 'and were there any sexual problems?'

109. Which cartoon character said: 'eat my shorts'?

110. Who accepted her Grammy award with a speech thanking her husband and 'God because **She** makes everything possible'?

111. What do the satellite TV channel initials CNN stand for?

112. Out of the five *Death Wish* films, how many have been directed by Michael Winner?

113. Who dressed up as The Penguin in the film *Batman Returns*?

114. In which film is the last line: 'It's your kids, Marty, something's got to be done about your kids'?

115. Which composer wrote 'On Hearing The First Cuckoo in Spring'?

116. Which American actor was described by a film critic as 'Perhaps the most hostile of all American actors'?

117. Who directed and starred in the 1993 film version of *Much Ado about Nothing?*

118. Which 1987 film starred Anne Bancroft as an

American writer and Anthony Hopkins as a bookseller?

119. Membership of which American organisation is limited to the direct lineal descendants of soldiers or others of the Revolutionary period?

120. What is the more common name for the instrument called an English horn?

121. Which author is usually credited with writing the first modern detective story?

122. Who wrote *Eugene Onegin?*

123. What does an etymologist study?

124. Which 1985 Steven Spielberg film co-starred Oprah Winfrey?

125. *Coming Up Roses* was a subtitled film. Which language were the actors speaking?

126. Which 1985 film starred Madonna and Rosanna Arquette?

127. In 1990, what happened to the sets from *Back to the Future*, *The Sting* and *Oscar?*

128. In *Oscar*, who played Sylvester Stallone's father?

129. Which 1992 film had characters with colours for surnames? Another mark for anyone who can think of another movie where the same applied.

130. Which actress is Tippi Hedren's daughter?

131. Which actress worked as a bricklayer and in a mortuary?

132. Which actor despised being called 'the new Marlon Brando'?

133. What connects *Chariots of Fire* to Harrods?

134. Which scriptwriter was once a policeman on *Z-Cars*?

135. Which Tarzan also won five gold medals for swimming in the Olympics?

136. What is the most frequently shown movie on American television?

137. Of which film did Robert Redford say: 'It was the most consistent fun of any film I've ever done'?

138. What classic film began as a playlet entitled *Still Life*?

139. What is the connection between Celia Johnson and James Bond?

140. In which film did Minnesota Fats and Fast Eddie meet?

141. Which two actors connect Cool Hand Luke and Butch Cassidy and the Sundance Kid?

142. What leading role did Robert Culp turn down in a popular soap?

143. John Forsythe got the role of Blake Carrington in *Dynasty* because the first choice stormed off the set in a tantrum. Who was it?

144. Who was offered the role of Butch Cassidy, turned it down only to be offered the role of the Sundance Kid and turned that down too?

145. Who refused the role of Crystal Carrington and still regrets it to this day?

146. After George Peppard, who was second choice to play Blake Carrington in *Dynasty*?

147. Which film star achieved her classic, gaunt looks by having her rear teeth removed?

148. Who insured his nose for a quarter of a million dollars?

149. Which American actor won Lassie in a poker game?

150. Which American comedy actors all took their stage names from a comic strip entitled *Mager's Monks*?

151. Who played the Odd Couple in the television series?

152. Which famous horror actor was actually born in Transylvania?

153. In which country was Patrick McGoohan born?

154. In which country was Olivia Newton-John born?

155. Which knighted British actor is of mixed Russian and Ethiopian descent?

156. In which country were Al Jolson, Irving Berlin and George Sanders all born?

157. If you know where Jack Lemmon was born, you'll know why his star was destined to rise. Where was it?

158. Which dancer married Robert Powell?

159. Which British artist sang 'The Man from Laramie'?

160. Judged on the number of weeks in the top twenty popular music charts, who are the two top acts?

161. Name any two musicians who formed The Quintet of the Hot Club of France.

162. What folk group's name means 'Family'?

163. Which poet wrote 'Sea Fever'?

164. Name any one of the Brontë sisters along with her male pen-name.

165. Which actor played Branwell Brontë in the 1970s television series?

166. Who did Nancy Sinatra sing with on *Did You Ever*?

167. Who sang 'Alfie'?

168. 'Always There' was sung by Marti Webb, which BBC series did the music come from?

169. Which brass band recorded 'The Floral Dance'?

170. Who successfully sued George Harrison for his release of 'My Sweet Lord'?

171. Following on from the previous question, what was the title of the song that Harrison was said to have used?

172. Who sang 'Minuetto Allegretto'?

173. In which Sheridan play are the characters of Sir Anthony Absolute and Lydia Languish?

174. Who is called the second Adam or the new Adam?

175. Who wrote *I Know Why The Caged Bird Sings*?

176. Which group of mythological travellers included Heracles, Orpheus, Peleus and Castor?

177. In the title of the song 'Auld Lang Syne', what does the Lang Syne mean?

178. Whose plays include *A Chorus of Disapproval* and *Season's Greetings*?

179. Who was the first English professional female writer and served Charles II as a spy?

180. In the Bible, who was called 'the beloved physician'?

181. In what year was the King James version of the Bible published? (Allow 10 years either side.)

182. In which Dickens novel does John Peerybingle appear?

183. Which occultist was the subject of Somerset Maugham's novel *The Magician*?

184. Which writer, best known for his children's stories and poems, wrote the screenplays for *You Only Live Twice* and *Chitty Chitty Bang Bang*?

185. What is the name of the twelve novel sequence written by Anthony Powell?

186. What was Dickens's final and unfinished novel?

187. What do the initials of E M Forster stand for?

188. Name any two of the Four Horsemen of the Apocalypse.

189. Which playwright wrote *Ghosts*?

190. How many comic operas did Gilbert and Sullivan write?

191. What was the name of Sherlock Holmes's brother?

192. Which British poet was also a Jesuit priest?

193. Who wrote a volume of poems entitled *A Shropshire Lad*?

194. Who directed *2001: A Space Odyssey*, *The Shining* and *Full Metal Jacket*?

195. Who wrote *Rosemary's Baby*, *Stepford Wives* and *The Boys from Brazil*?

196. What village did Miss Marple live in?

197. What do these poets have in common, A Austin, H Pye, and Cecil Day Lewis?

198. In which century was the position of Poet Laureate first officially named as such?

199. What is the imaginary Central European kingdom in *The Prisoner of Zenda*?

200. What were Gram, Morglay, Phillipan and Flamberge?

201. Who was Uther Pendragon?

202. Which poet and dramatist wrote *The Selfish Giant*?

203. Who is buried at St Paul's Cathedral under a memorial stone that reads 'If thou seekest a monument, gaze around'?

204. Which French painter joined Picasso in creating the Cubist movement?

205. What is the name for the network of small cracks

which appear in a painting when the pigment or varnish has become brittle?

206. What is the term given to a picture consisting of two parts facing each other?

207. What is the name of the world famous French tapestry manufacturer?

208. What is a lay figure?

209. What is the more familiar name for serigraphy?

210. Which artist provided the original illustrations for *Alice in Wonderland*?

211. What do J M W Turner's initials stand for?

212. What is the name of the chief public art gallery in Florence?

213. Which museum was developed from the profits of the Great Exhibition?

214. Albert Campion is the detective creation of which author?

215. In which story is Amyas Leigh the hero?

216. In which famous poem do Death and Life-in-Death play dice aboard a skeleton ship?

217. Name the Three Musketeers.

218. *The Bell Jar* was originally published under

the pen-name of Victoria Lucas. What was the author's real name?

219. A C Benson wrote the words for *Land of Hope and Glory*. For what literary works was his brother famous?

220. Which American writer disappeared in Mexico during 1913?

221. What was the real name of George Orwell?

222. Who was the author of *Madame Bovary*?

223. Which broadcaster and novelist was brought up in Cumberland and educated at Wadham College, Oxford?

224. Which novel is narrated by Charles Ryder?

225. Which book title has come to describe a deadlocked situation?

226. How old was the poet Thomas Chatterton when he died?

227. Under what name was Mrs Max Mallowan better known?

228. What was Mudie's?

229. Which poet published volumes entitled *Village Minstrel* and *The Shepherd's Calendar*?

230. What has been called The Fourth Estate?

231. Whose autobiography was entitled *The Story of My Experiments with Truth*?

232. What was founded in 1831 as a club in which 'actors and men of education and refinement might meet on equal terms'?

233. In modern usage, what is a gazetteer?

234. What type of art is associated with Kate Greenaway?

235. Which royal mistress's son was created Duke of St Albans?

236. Which American author's books feature an amoral anti-hero called Tom Ripley?

237. In what year was *Mein Kampf* published?

238. What is the term for books printed before the 16th century?

239. Who wrote *I am a Camera*, later to form the basis of *Cabaret*?

240. Who spends her early years in Lowood Institution and then becomes a governess at Thornfield Hall?

241. Who wrote *Three Men in a Boat*?

242. Which economist wrote *A General Theory of Employment, Interest and Money*?

243. What was the occupation of Francis Kilvert whose diaries were published in 1938?

244. Which years were covered by Samuel Pepys' diaries?

245. Which of Coleridge's poems was never finished because, according to the poet, he was interrupted by 'a person from Porlock'?

246. Which literary prize has been awarded to Winston Churchill, Ernest Hemingway, William Golding and Saul Bellow?

247. Which modern American author has written *The War Between The Tates* and *Imaginary Friends?*

248. Jonathan Aycliffe is a contemporary ghost story writer, under what other name does he write?

249. Who is the hero in *Around the World in 80 Days*?

250. Under which pseudonym does David John Moore Cornwell write?

251. Which 19th century writer was one of twenty children of a stockbroker and worked as a zoological draughtsman?

252. One of the daughters of the Earl of Bessborough wrote *Glenarvon* but was more famous for her infatuation with another writer, who was she?

253. Which Cambridge college is the home of Pepys' diaries?

254. Which present day national newspaper was founded in 1821?

255. Which writer created Chief Detective Inspector Roderick Alleyn?

256. In which novel do you find Tom and Maggie Tulliver?

257. What is Ogham?

258. *A Better Class of Person* is the first volume of the autobiography of which British playwright?

259. Which poet of the First World War died one week before the Armistice?

260. Whose passionate violin playing gave rise to the notion that he possessed supernatural powers?

261. Who directed the 1993 film *The Piano*?

262. Who is the author of the *Discworld* series of science fiction novels?

263. When is Quasimodo Sunday?

264. Which author, chiefly remembered for his children's stories, was married to Trotsky's secretary?

265. Who wrote *A Taste of Honey?*

266. Under which single-name pseudonym did H H Munro write?

267. Regius professorships have been awarded at Oxford and Cambridge since the 16th century – name any two subjects covered by them?

268. Who was the novelist wife of Harold Nicolson?

269. In which novel is Holden Caulfield the central character?

270. Which hit musical of recent years includes the songs 'Castle in the Clouds' and 'Do You Hear The People Sing'?

271. In which century was an act passed requiring a printer to give three copies of any works printed by him to the Stationers Company?

272. Which contentious artifact is claimed to be the object previously known as the Mandylion?

273. What was Zsa Zsa Gabor's original first name?

274. For which film was this the advertising slogan: 'Sister, sister, oh so fair, why is there blood all over your hair'?

275. Which actress was known as America's Sweetheart?

276. Which historical character has been portrayed by Kenneth Haigh, Ian Holm and Claude Rains?

277. What was the name of the aristocratic family in *Kind Hearts and Coronets*?

278. Which musical features songs called 'The Greatest Star of All', 'As If We Never Said Goodbye', and 'This time next Year'?

279. How many Oscars did *Singin' in the Rain* win?

280. Who played Mr Chips in the 1939 film of *Goodbye, Mr Chips*?

281. Which recent musical work comprises eight movements including 'War', 'School', 'Wedding' and 'Work'?

282. Supply the final line of this song chorus: 'England swings like a pendulum do / Bobbies on bicycles two by two / Westminster Abbey, The Tower Big Ben / . . .'

283. Who won thirty-two Oscars?

284. Which female artist painted the charge of the Royal Scots Greys at Waterloo entitled *Scotland for Ever!*?

285. One of the Marx brothers never appeared with the others on film, who was he? (Accept first name or stage name.)

286. Which author wrote under the following pseudonyms: Anthony Morton, Robert Caine Frazer and Margaret Cooke?

287. In which play would you find Donna Lucia d'Alvadorez, Lord Fancourt Babberley and Jack Chesney?

288. How was William Dukinfield better known?

289. Who was the composer of the theme and incidental music for the *Inspector Morse* series?

290. Musically, what connects Caroline Alice, Richard Baxter Townshend and Richard Penrose Arnold?

291. In the art world how did Hans Van Meegeren achieve fame?

292. Alice B Toklas – what did the 'B' stand for?

293. Which detective was assisted by a young man called Tinker and a bloodhound called Pedro?

294. What was odd about the 18th century play *Vortigern and Rowena*?

295. Who was Greyfriars Bobby?

296. Which coveted role, in a film that has yet to be made (1994), has been offered to Madonna, Meryl Streep, Michelle Pfeiffer and Liza Minnelli?

297. Which Shakespearian character says: 'Tell the truth and shame the devil'?

298. Which poet and playwright penned the lines: 'God's in his heaven and all's right with the world'?

299. Which stage musical includes songs called 'Early in the Morning', 'Messy Bessy' and 'Don't Let the Sun Catch You Crying'?

300. Name all three films in the *Star Wars* series.

301. Name any four of the seven deadly sins.

302. What were the names of The Righteous Brothers?

303. Who sang the official theme of the Barcelona Olympics?

304. Who sang the British entry in the 1994 Eurovision Song Contest?

305. Who composed 'The Kingdom and Coronation Ode'?

306. Name two of the Titans.

307. Who wrote the opera *The Touchstone*?

308. What was Voltaire's real name?

309. When is Walpurgis Night?

310. Which group's song 'Don't Stop Thinking About Tomorrow' became the theme for the Clinton presidential campaign?

311. What is unusual about the book *Caressing Picasso*?

312. Which T V series finally ended in May 1993 after 275 episodes?

313. Which film star died August 16 1993?

314. What is the title of the book that is the sequel to *Gone with the Wind* and (for an extra point) who is its author?

315. Where is rock idol Jim Morrison buried?

316. Who wrote *Under The Eye of The Clock*?

317. A New York theatre critic said that it was: 'impoverished of artistic personality and passion'. Which musical show was he talking about?

318. Which leading British choreographer died in August 1988?

319. Why was Koo Stark awarded damages of £300,000 against the *Sunday People* in November 1988?

320. Who played Anthony Blunt in the Alan Bennett play *Single Spies*?

321. Whose performance in *City Slickers* won him the Best Supporting Actor award in the 1992 Oscars?

322. Who was the first Caribbean writer to receive the Nobel Prize for literature?

323. Which comic book character was killed off in November 1992?

324. Which Parisian night-spot was forced to close down in December 1992?

325. In which opera does a faithful wife disguise herself as a man in order to free her husband from prison?

326. In which opera does a Prince free the daughter of a Queen with the aid of an enchanted instrument?

327. Who played the part of Tchaikovsky in *The Music Lovers*?

328. *Song without End* was a film in which Dirk Bogarde took the part of which composer?

329. What does the musical term *mezza voce* mean?

330. What does the musical term *bravura* mean?

331. How many children did J S Bach have?

332. Which composer was Wagner's father-in-law?

333. What nationality was the composer Giovanni Pergolesi?

334. What nationality was the composer Carl Nielsen?

335. Who composed *The Dream of Gerontius*?

336. Who composed *Belshazzar's Feast*?

337. Of which composer did someone say: 'He has some very good moments, but some very bad quarters-of-an-hour'?

338. Which American composer had a successful insurance business?

339. Debussy's *La Mer* was inspired by the sea. Which sea did he look at whilst he wrote it?

340. Which composer, more well known for lighter works, wrote the tune for the hymn 'Onward Christian Soldiers'?

341. Who wrote the tune for the carol 'Hark, the Herald Angels Sing'?

342. In which year were both Bach and Handel born?

343. What was the real name of the English composer Peter Warlock?

344. Which of these is not one of Holst's Planets: Uranus, Pluto, Neptune, Venus, Mercury?

345. Which 20th century composer wrote a piece called '4 minutes 33 seconds'?

346. Musically speaking, what would you do with a serpent?

347. Of which composer did someone say: 'Hats off, gentlemen – a genius'?

348. In which opera would you find The Dark Fiddler?

349. Prince Orlofsky is a character in which opera?

350. Which composer wrote the music for *On The Waterfront*?

351. Which composer wrote the music for the 1942 film version of *Hamlet*?

352. Which composer was awarded the Military Cross and was killed aged thirty-one whilst fighting on the Somme?

353. Which composer died after being crushed under a falling bookcase?

354. Who invented the metronome?

355. Who wrote *The Cunning Little Vixen*?

356. Which composer went deaf in 1874 and died insane?

357. Which 19th century artist is famous for his black and white drawings of fantastic and erotic subjects?

358. What was George Eliot's real name?

359. What do T S Eliot's initials stand for?

360. How did Dr Johnson define a lexicographer?

361. Which modern artist painted *Peter Getting Out of Nick's Pool*?

362. Jean-François Champollion was a French linguist. What is his best known achievement?

363. William Sydney Porter was an American writer who began to write stories whilst in prison for embezzlement. He wrote under a pseudonym, what was it?

364. According to some, the Greek playwright Aeschylus was killed by a tortoise, how?

365. Which science fiction writer published his first six books under the pseudonym Paul French?

366. What came out of a meeting between Percy Shelley, George Byron, Dr John Polidori and Mary Wollstonecraft?

367. Who was responsible for these lines: 'Twas the

night before Christmas and all through the house, not a creature was stirring, not even a mouse'?

368. How many copies of the Gutenberg Bible were published? (Allow any answer within 50.)

369. Still with the Gutenberg Bible, how many copies are still extant?

370. Which composer said: 'Give me a laundry list and I'll set it to music'?

371. An organistrum was the forerunner of which instrument?

372. What type of ballet is a *ballo a cavallo*?

373. Apart from being writers, what do Shakespeare and Miguel Cervantes have in common?

374. What items were used by Napoleon as ration cards during the French Revolution?

375. Which famous singer was quoted as saying that rock and roll was phony, false and written and played for the most part by cretinous goons?

376. Which is the only Shakespeare play that does not have a song in it?

377. Which writer suffered from epilepsy and created five characters who suffered with the disease?

378. What bodily malformation did Daniel Defoe have?

379. On an examination after his death, which poet was discovered to have clubbed feet and legs withered to the knee?

380. What is a wyvern?

381. What is xylography?

382. Where did Elizabeth Taylor host the party for her sixtieth birthday?

383. What opened its doors for the first time on April 12 1992?

384. Which award did Michael Caine receive in the Queen's Birthday Honours list?

385. On September 22 1955 the first television commercial appeared on our screens, what was the product being advertised?

386. What was the name of The Man in a Suitcase?

387. In the 1950s series *Colonel March of Scotland Yard* who played the Colonel?

388. In the television series of *Dragnet* who played Sergeant Joe Friday?

389. What hit comedy show of the fifties and early sixties starred David Kossoff and Peggy Mount?

390. Who was the chairman of the original Juke Box Jury?

391. Which actor turned down the role of James Bond and thus gave Sean Connery his big break?

392. Which programme was nicknamed 'TW3'?

393. Who played Rowdy Yates in *Rawhide*?

394. On *Ready, Steady, Go* who was Cathy McGowan's co-presenter?

395. Which Galton and Simpson show began life as a Comedy Playhouse production called *The Offer*?

396. Which catchphrase was coined by Janice Nicholls?

397. In the Homepride Flour commercials, what was the name of the chief flourgrader?

398. What was the name of the detective in *Public Eye*?

399. Name any two of the sons in *Thunderbirds*.

400. What was the name of Peter Cook and Dudley Moore's sixties comedy series?

401. Name any two of the Monkees.

402. Which children's programme was presented by Fred Dineage, Jack Hargreaves and Bunty James?

403. What did Barry Bucknell do?

404. Who presented *Animal Magic*?

405. In which series did Derek Nimmo play a curate?

406. In *The Avengers* what was the name of the female assistant who replaced Emma Peel?

407. What was the name of Eric Porter's character in *The Forsyte Saga*?

408. Who played Bernard Hedges in *Please Sir*?

409. In which series did Patrick Wymark take the part of John Wilder?

410. What was the name of the family in *A Family At War*?

411. Apart from being comedians, what do Dave Allen, Des O'Connor, Ted Rogers and Jimmy Tarbuck have in common?

412. Pentangle's 'Late Flight' was the theme tune for which drama series?

413. Which seventies crime series starred Tony Curtis and Roger Moore?

414. Who took the part of Sally Abbott in *Bless This House*?

415. In which series did Adam Faith play a petty criminal?

416. Name The Goodies.

417. What was Beryl's pet name for Geoffrey in *The Lovers*?

418. In *Coronation Street*, what was Emily's surname before her marriage to Ernie Bishop?

419. Who were the three 'characters' that appeared in *Rainbow* alongside Geoffrey Hayes?

420. On the Teletext service what does ORACLE stand for?

421. Which was the first royal wedding to be transmitted in colour?

422. Who sang and composed the theme tune for *No, Honestly*?

423. For which family did Mary Holland play the mother Katie?

424. Who said 'Sch, you know who'?

425. The creator of the original Hovis advert is also a top movie director, who is he?

426. In the T V costume drama *Edward the Seventh*, who played Queen Victoria?

427. In *The Good Life*, what were the first names of all four characters?

428. Who was the eccentric scientist presenter of *Don't Ask Me*?

429. Who hosted *Multi-Coloured Swap Shop*?

430. Which Dr Who was the longest in the role?

431. Which actress was the female lead in *The Cuckoo Waltz*?

432. In the seventies television film *Jesus of Nazareth* who played Mary?

433. When Norman Stanley Fletcher left Slade Prison what comedy series did he walk into?

434. Which series had male characters called Ben, Russell, Adam and Leonard?

435. Which character in the *Liver Birds* had the same surname as the family in *Bread*?

436. In *Lillie* who played the part of Oscar Wilde?

437. Which actor moved into Grantley Manor when Mrs Fforbes Hamilton was forced to move out?

438. Which series is set in the fictional village of Glendarroch?

439. Which stately home became the fictional home of the Flyte family in *Brideshead Revisited*?

440. Who described her time in a soap opera as 'a long and lovely velvet rut'?

441. What was the name of the dog in *Hart to Hart*?

442. In *The Towering Inferno* what did they finally do to put the fire out?

443. What publication sells twenty-eight million copies worldwide for each issue?

444. In *High Society* what is the name of Grace Kelly's character?

445. Two films end with the main character reaching for a butterfly. Can you name either of them?

446. 'He's so adorable, I could just tuck him under my arm and take him home' – which British star was this American columnist referring to?

447. The presenter of *Out of Town* died early in 1994 – who was he?

448. Why did *Countdown* claim a unique place in TV history?

449. Which actor played Reilly – Ace of Spies?

450. Name three of the so-called Famous Five in at the launch of TV-am.

451. Still with Famous Fives – what were the first names of Enid Blyton's Famous Five?

452. Which series began life as a one-off play called *Woodentop*?

453. Who wrote *The Thorn Birds* on which the TV series was based?

454. In *The A-Team*, what did B A Baracus's initials stand for?

455. When Elsie Tanner finally left *Coronation Street*, which country did she supposedly emigrate to?

456. What is the name of Arkwright's nephew in *Open All Hours*?

457. Which Fleet Street satire featured Robert Hardy in his first comedy role?

458. In which year was the Band Aid concert staged?

459. Who played Reece Dinsdale's father in *Home To Roost*?

460. Who is the author of the *Lovejoy* books?

461. Who was the first chairman in *A Question of Sport*?

462. Which Brewer sponsored some of the *Inspector Morse* series?

463. Which two characters were replaced by different actors in *Bread*?

464. Which popular series finished with the only original cast member driving off into the sunset in a sports car with her new lover?

465. How did Sharon Maughan and Tony Head become better known?

466. In what drama did Ray McAnally play the part of a left-wing Prime Minister?

467. Who were the three male actors in *Three Men and a Baby*?

468. Which pop star is the voice for Thomas the Tank Engine?

469. What three animals lay down together in front of a coal fire in a Real Fire commercial?

470. Which detective was played by George Baker?

471. Which children's series featuring Jim Henson's puppets was set in a lighthouse?

472. Who worked for C J at Sunshine Desserts?

473. Which actress played Bridget and Behaved Badly?

474. Which actress, notoriously famous for attacking Russell Harty, appeared in Roger Moore's last Bond film?

475. Which playwright is married to Maureen Lipman?

476. Who played the new captain in the re-vamped *Star Trek*?

477. In the Jeeves and Wooster books, what is Jeeves's first name?

478. On which Radio Four spoof panel game do they play an even spoofier game called Mornington Crescent?

479. In which pop song does a jester sing to a king and queen in a coat he's borrowed from James Dean?

480. Within five thousand, how many videos were sent in to *You've Been Framed* for the first series?

481. What do the following situation comedies have in common: *Second Thoughts*, *Up The Garden Path* and *After Henry*?

482. What relatively short-lived series was described by the *Guardian* as 'going straight for the young

drunk vote with a directness which leaves you winded'?

483. When *Prime Suspect* won the 1991 BAFTA award what did four of the seven jurors insist they had voted for instead?

484. In what series taken from a Melvyn Bragg novel was a middle-aged bank manager more than platonically involved with a teenage lover called Bernadette?

485. Who killed Laura Palmer?

486. What name was given to BSB's satellite 'dish'?

487. In what series would you find a pair of ornithologists called Brenda and Malcolm?

488. Who played the warring parents in *Kramer Vs Kramer*?

489. Which TV presenter became MP for Chester in 1992?

490. Who played an agony aunt in, appropriately enough, *Agony*?

491. In *Sorry* what was the name of Ronnie Corbett's character?

492. What programme dominated the television screens on 29th July 1981?

493. What character did Daniel Travanti play in *Hill Street Blues*?

494. Which character said: 'I could do that – gissa job'?

495. Which animation firm produced *Wind in the Willows*?

496. In which BBC series did Ray Brookes play card games for high stakes?

497. How many spin-off series came out of *Man About the House*?

498. When the first Mrs Bellamy died on the *Titanic*, who became the second Mrs Bellamy?

499. Who were the two in *Two's Company*?

500. On the opening titles of which show are the following lines superimposed: 'the women come and go and talk of Michelangelo'?

501. Which BBC music show was presented by 'Whispering' Bob Harris?

502. Which BBC series' theme music is entitled 'I wish that I knew how it felt to be free'?

503. Which actors became Starsky and Hutch?

504. Who kept the streets safe for inhabitants of Manhattan's 13th Precinct?

505. In the Peter Seger song, what were the little boxes on the hillside made out of?

506. From which musical did these song lines come:

'Why can't they be like we were, perfect in every way, Oh, what's the matter with kids today'?

507. What part did Joel Grey take in *Cabaret*?

508. Which Stephen King novel was a big hit on screen but flopped dramatically and expensively when turned into a musical?

509. Which seventies teen idol took over from Cliff Richard in the musical *Time*?

510. Half of which pop group collaborated with Tim Rice to produce *Chess*?

511. What was Tim Rice studying at university when he teamed up with Andrew Lloyd-Webber?

512. Who chose a stage name to replace his real name of Michael Patrick Dumble-Smith?

513. Which actor from the *Carry On* series of films co-wrote the Seekers' hit 'Georgy Girl'?

514. Which female singer was the first white British person to secure a deal with the Tamla Motown label?

515. In the 1973 production of *Grease*, which now well-known American actor took the part of Danny Zuko?

516. Which British actress and singer was the niece of Nancy Astor?

517. Who sang the theme song from *The Thomas Crown Affair*?

518. For which rather disastrous musical did Andrew Lloyd-Webber team up with Alan Ayckbourn?

519. Which seventies teen idol took the lead in the Canadian production of *Joseph and His Amazing Technicolour Dreamcoat*?

520. Apart from the fact that Judy Garland was in the film, what other connection does Liza Minnelli have with *The Wizard Of Oz*?

521. Which soap opera did Elaine Paige appear in?

522. What ambition, unlikely ever to be fulfilled, is shared by Tim Rice, Jeffrey Archer and Colin Dexter?

523. What was the fictional town setting for *Howard's Way*?

524. Before the television success of the *Inspector Morse* stories, what make of car did the Morse of Colin Dexter's books drive?

525. In the mini-series *Murderers Among Us* who took the part of Simon Wiesenthal?

526. Which ITV newsreader retired in 1989?

527. J M W Turner left his £140,000 fortune to establish a charity – who were the intended beneficiaries?

528. Who composed 'Rule Britannia'?

529. 'If I should die, think only this of me . . .', what is the title of the poem?

530. Which author, famous for his children's works, also wrote *The Red House Mystery*, and *Mr Pim Passes By*?

531. British author Alexander Cruden is known for what famous standard reference work?

532. Which art collection is situated in Home House, London?

533. Antonio Allegri was an artist far better known under another name, what was it?

534. What is the common name given to the handwriting style known as English round hand?

535. Which author wrote *The Deerslayer*, *The Pathfinder*, and *The Prairie*?

536. During the Reign of Terror who made the death masks of the severed heads produced by Madam Guillotine?

537. Which world famous instrument hails from Cremona in Italy?

538. What did Rex Harrison and Sammy Davis Jnr have in common?

539. The American cult movie, *They Shoot Horses, Don't They?* centred on a teenage craze, what was it?

540. Which dance takes its name from the Czech for half a step?

541. Samuel Richardson's novel *Pamela* and Laurence Sternes's *A Sentimental Journey through France and Italy* share a singular distinction. What is it?

542. What was first installed at the Palais Royale saloon in San Francisco in November 1889?

543. What is the first statue in England to be made of aluminium?

544. Which infamous lady's stage name was the Malay for the sun?

545. Whose will left his wife 'the second best bed' of the house?

546. Which musical instrument was invented circa 1710 by Batholomeo Christofori?

547. In the film *To Have And Have Not*, Lauren Bacall appears to sing but who dubbed for her voice?

548. The surname of the famous poet Omar Khayam indicates his proper trade. What was it?

549. The biblical books of Obadiah, Philemon and Jude have one thing in common. What is it?

550. Rather ironically, a 9th precinct house served as the setting for a famous American cop film. What was the title?

551. Who served as the model-type for Walt Disney when penning his original cartoon character of Tinkerbell for *Peter Pan*?

552. Mel Blanc, voice of Bugs Bunny and many others, was seriously allergic to what?

553. What do Julie Christie and Joanna Lumley have in common?

554. What is inscribed on W C Fields's gravestone?

555. What do the following have in common: Ernest Hemingway, tennis star Bill Tilden, Oscar Wilde and Thomas Wolfe?

556. The haggis is not a Scottish invention, so who introduced it to the British Isles?

557. In 1983, a new toy was launched. It was so popular in America that in transit thefts were stopped by armoured car delivery. To prevent a riot Woolworth's in Lawrence, Kansas placed the last seven toys in a bank vault and held a lottery to select last purchasers. What was the toy?

558. In a certain runaway movie success the robotic star was given a nickname by the film crew. That nickname was Bruce – what was the film?

559. In what year was the first commercial LP released?

560. Which novel was adapted to become the musical *Hello Dolly*?

561. What disorder forced Vaslav Nijinsky to retire from ballet at age of twenty-nine?

562. When film star Mary Pickford married for the

second time which other film star became her husband?

563. Whereabouts did the first British cinema open?

564. Which artiste was known as 'Two Ton Tessie'?

565. Which popular pub name is a corruption of 'God Encompasseth Us'?

566. What is the plural of mongoose?

567. In Latin *me transmitte sursum, Caledoni!* represents which well-known phrase?

568. Which form of writing is named for its wedge shaped letters?

569. In England, holding the thumb and forefinger in a circle means perfect or spot-on. What does it signify in Japan?

570. Which quaint old English custom is named after an African people?

571. Which newspaper group bought the *Observer* in 1993?

572. Which three opera singers are connected with the 1990 World Cup?

573. Which film starred Bill Murray as a weatherman caught in an endlessly repeating day?

574. On which writer's early life is the opera *Baa Baa Black Sheep* based?

575. How many thousand dollars did a thirty second

commercial cost screened during the final episode of *Cheers*?

576. Which scientist is referred to in the Beatles song 'The Fool On The Hill'?

577. In 1993, what type of Bronze Age item was discovered in Dover whilst modern sewers were being enlarged?

578. Which country sued which other country for the return of the 'Lydian Hoard' – a collection of gold and silver vessels and jewellery?

579. Which rock musician had children called Dweezil, Ahmet and Diva?

580. Which two actors played Nick and Nora Charles in a series of six films?

581. Which author of historical novels died at sea between Athens and Port Said?

582. Who was a Passing Stranger with Sarah Vaughan?

583. Which comedian penned an autobiography called *A Clown Too Many*?

584. In *The Incredible Hulk*, who played the Hulk?

585. Which member of the British aristocracy was immortalised in Cole Porter's song 'You're The Top'?

586. Who wrote the book on which the film *Jurassic Park* was based?

587. A Yellow Pages advert was responsible for creating a book and author that did not actually exist. What was the name of the book and the author?

588. Which famous arts festival was attacked by its director for turning into a 'third rate circus'?

589. In which city did the Tate Gallery open a new wing during 1988?

590. Since it first appeared in 1884, how many editions have there been of the *Oxford English Dictionary*?

591. Which actor aged dramatically overnight and then danced on a giant keyboard in *Big*?

592. In which film does Jack Nicholson endlessly write 'all work and no play makes Jack a dull boy'?

593. In 1940, Picasso sent his picture *Guernica* to New York for safekeeping, refusing to allow it back into Spain until democracy was restored. How many years later did it finally take its place in Madrid's Prado Museum?

594. Which dancer became a Bavarian Countess and was also known for her liaisons with Franz Liszt and Alexandre Dumas?

595. Who played the Cowardly Lion in the *Wizard of Oz*?

596. Known by the Germans as the Battle of Skagerrak, how was this battle known by the British?

597. What leisure item, enjoyed by children and adults alike, was devised in 1762 by an English printer called John Spilsbury?

598. On October 11 1963, France lost two of its most famous artistic and cultural figures, who were they?

599. Which TV star was critically injured during storms which swept the country during January 1990?

600. Which city was City of Drama in 1994?

601. In 1990, what city began its year as Cultural Capital of Europe?

602. In 1991, according to a government survey, who toppled Enid Blyton from her spot as the most read children's author?

603. Who did Jeremy Irons portray when he won the Best Actor Oscar in 1991?

604. The 19th century periodical *The Examiner* carried a banner on its cover explaining why its cost was 7d: 3½ pence was for print and paper, what was the other 3½ pence for?

605. Which role do the following actors have in common: Donald Sutherland, George Burns and Richard Pryor?

606. Which writer said: 'My work has no message

for humanity and unless I discover one soon humanity is likely to remain a message short'?

607. In Betjeman's poem about Joan Hunter Dunn, what town is 'heavy with bells' at nine o'clock?

608. Name either of the two radio stations that provided the first legal competition for BBC Radio.

609. In the early seventies, which award-winning children's programme was denounced by the Soviet Union for being 'imperialistic'?

610. What is the name of the lion in *The Lion, The Witch and The Wardrobe*?

611. London's South Bank is home to a museum devoted to the history of cinema and television. What is its name?

612. A ballerina with the Kirov company defected in 1970. Who was she?

613. 'Tiger! Tiger! burning bright / In the forests of the night' – what comes next?

614. Which cartoon character made a debut in *The Wise Little Hen*?

615. Who succeeded Sir Arnold Bax as Master of the Queen's Music?

616. The E Street band were the backing group for which rock star?

617. What film was Elvis Presley making shortly

before his wedding and during his honeymoon?

618. What was the first record to be released on Richard Branson's Virgin label?

619. Which writer left £500,000 to endow a Chair of Parapsychology at Edinburgh University?

620. Daugherty, DiMaggio – who completes the trio?

621. Which feminist author wrote about her experiences as a Bunny Girl?

622. 'If you want to know anything about me, just look at the surface of my paintings. It's all there, there's nothing more'. Which artist said this?

623. Characters from John Gay's *Beggars Opera* were included in another updated, operatic version of the story. What was the opera?

624. We all know The Archers meet for a drink at the Bull, but what is the other rival pub mentioned in the series?

625. Who cut Samson's hair?

626. Name the two main Russian newspapers. One point each and for a further two points what do the two titles mean?

627. In the original texts of the Bible there is a tale of a character presented with a long-sleeved garment. How is this character and his outfit known today?

628. In Greek mythology who was the god of sleep?

629. In Ian Fleming's novels, the dictatorial 'M' was based on who?

630. In the 19th century the parliamentary seat of Kitley in Devon was represented by the unfortunately named John Pollexfen Bastard. He became the inspiration for a popular TV character – name him.

631. In *Blackadder*, the much put upon character of Baldrick has a name describing an item of Elizabethan dress. By what name is it better known?

632. Rather unflatteringly, Robert Louis Stevenson wrote a book whilst on his honeymoon touring Europe. Even less flattering was the title, what was it?

633. The novel *Catriona* is a little known sequel to which much more famous work?

634. In the 1954 classic *The Glen Miller Story*, James Stewart played Glen Miller but who took the part of Louis Armstrong?

635. Still with *The Glenn Miller Story*, the actor who played Miller's friend and pianist Chummy MacGregor appeared in *MASH*. Which character does he play?

636. Who first burst upon the entertainment scene with the stage name Buster Keys?

637. Where do we find first mention of a runcible spoon?

638. Why did no black jazz musicians make records in New Orleans in the jazz era?

639. Bathsheba of Bible fame had a son who was big in the mining business. Who was he?

640. To an Australian, what is a jumbuck?

641. How many letters are there in the Greek alphabet?

642. Which playing card is known as the Curse of Scotland?

643. An actress better known for her role in *Terms of Endearment* contributed towards the voice of ET in Steven Spielberg's film of that name. Who is she?

644. Which famous sculptor and wood-carver was made master carver to George I and most famously worked on St Paul's Cathedral, Petworth House in Sussex and Burghley House in Lincolnshire?

645. Who painted *The Monarch of the Glen* and sculpted the lions which sit at the base of Nelson's Column?

646. When we speak of Michelangelo we are actually using his Christian name. What was his surname?

647. In the 1870s, which art critic accused the painter Whistler of 'flinging a pot of paint in the public face'?

648. How many works of sculpture or architecture by Leonardo Da Vinci are extant?

649. What word meaning 'likeness' is applied to an image of a saint or other holy personage?

650. Which famous painter usually signed his paintings as 'Pietro Pauolo'?

SCIENCE, INDUSTRY AND TECHNOLOGY

1. Which element has the symbol La?
2. Which element derives its name from the German for a goblin?
3. What is the name of the natural satellite which orbits closest to Saturn?
4. Milton's reaction is a test for what substance?
5. What will have been established to exist when a machine passes the Turning Test?
6. What do ROM and RAM stand for?
7. What does the acronym INTELSAT stand for?
8. What is constructed using the Isherwood system?

9. Approximately how many million years did the Jurassic period last for?

10. What is a katathermometer?

11. Where are the Langerhans islets?

12. What name is given to the time slot during which a spacecraft must be launched to best achieve its given mission trajectory?

13. Which creatures suffer from a disease known as limberneck?

14. What is the popular name for nitrous oxide?

15. In the building trade, what is the term for a vertical scroll at one end of a hand-rail?

16. Pellagra is a disease caused by deficiency in which vitamin?

17. What is the common name for nyctalopia?

18. Ormolu is an alloy of which metals?

19. What is an orrery?

20. What is the name given to the hypothetical supercontinent which consisted of all the present continents before they split up?

21. What does REM stand for?

22. How did Mary Mallon achieve fame?

23. Pedology is the study of what substance?

24. In space travel, what is a perigee?

25. What is the common name for Pertussis?

26. Name the two natural satellites of Mars.

27. Name any two of the four Galilean satellites of Jupiter.

28. What is the name for the hypothetical planet inside the orbit of Mercury?

29. What name is given to the technology dedicated to reducing the observable characteristics of military aircraft and missiles?

30. How many neck vertebrae does the giraffe have?

31. A computer programming language was named in honour of Byron's daughter, what was her full name.

32. What does an entomologist study?

33. In telecommunications, what is the silent period?

34. Blaise Pascal invented a machine that could add and subtract, in what year did it go on sale? (Allow ten years either side.)

35. When did Humphrey Davy invent the safety lamp? (Allow five years either side.)

36. Eugene Ely was the first person to perform what feat of aviation?

37. Which American firm was the first to manufacture nylon?

38. What do the following have in common, hoover, escalator and fridge?

39. Who was the first author to type a manuscript for a publisher?

40. What famous structure comprises 10 million bricks, 6,400 windows and is visible from 80 kilometres out to sea?

41. Who said: 'I don't give a damn for the invention, the dimes are what I'm after'?

42. For what research did James Watson, Francis Crick and Maurice Wilkins share a Nobel prize in 1962?

43. What invention arose from a country walk taken by George de Mestral in the early 1950s?

44. On the average male, approximately how many thousand bristles are cut off during shaving?

45. Which country built the world's first motorway? Bonus point for correct decade.

46. What common item was first marketed in America under the name Rectigraph?

47. Sales of what item went from 51 in 1903, to 90,000 the following year?

48. In the thirties, the poet John Masefield and the actress Sybil Thorndike were judges in a contest to find what?

49. Which was the first London Underground station to bring escalators into public service?

50. Which household item was first demonstrated in the laboratories of Bing Crosby Enterprises in 1952?

51. Prototypes for which car were produced with the financial backing of Hitler?

52. What modern innovation claimed a Turkish businessman as its first victim in the UK?

53. How many drams are there in one ounce?

54. What system of weights uses grains, scruples and drachms?

55. How many pounds are there in a ton?

56. How many yards are there in a rod, pole or perch?

57. What were a Carolus, a Jacobus, a Joannes and an angel?

58. Within a thousand yards, how many yards are there in a Hungarian mile?

59. Which linear measurement takes its name from its being set by one thousand double paces as taken by a Roman legionnaire travelling at standard march rate?

60. Boudoir, elephant, admiral and colombier were all sizes of what?

61. What is the name for the part of a solid figure left after the top part has been cut off on a plane parallel to the base?

62. How many pecks in a bushel?

63. What bird was held sacred by the Egyptians?

64. What was a trebuchet?

65. What did Cornelis Drebbel invent?

66. What order of mammals does the armadillo belong to?

67. What is an abyssal plain?

68. Which body of water has a mean depth of 4,280 metres?

69. Which of Newton's laws of motion states that a body moving at constant speed in a straight line will keep on moving in a straight line at a constant speed until acted upon by a force?

70. Who was the American astronomer who believed that there were irrigation ditches and vegetation on Mars?

71. In which century was the first London Bridge constructed?

72. Whereabouts was the oldest known key discovered?

73. Who built the Forth Bridge?

74. Who was tried by the Inquisition in Rome in 1633?

75. Who discovered Nitroglycerin?

76. Topographically speaking, what is an erg?

77. Where was the first American battery powered automobile built?

78. Who was the inventor of the storage battery?

79. What is cryosurgery?

80. Whereabouts in Italy were the first two botanical gardens founded?

81. In 1616, who announced observations on the circulation of the blood?

82. Within ten years, when was the existence of different blood groups discovered?

83. What were the forenames of the Montgolfier brothers?

84. What is anthropology?

85. What is adobe?

86. What substance was used to make gaskets in the first nuclear bomb?

87. What were Colossus Mark 1 and Mark 2?

88. What did American physicist Willy Higinbotham invent in 1958?

89. In 1932, what did August Dvorak develop?

90. In computing, what is a WORM disk?

91. What is a VLSI chip?

92. Still with computing, what do the following abbreviations stand for: CPU, ALU, DOS, CAD, CAL, WIMP, WYSIWYG? (Half a mark each)

93. Three fields of employment carry the greatest risk of occupational injury. Name any one of them.

94. In the period from 1981–1991, AIDS killed 500,000 people. How many died from measles in that same period?

95. What gas ignited and caused the Hindenberg to crash in 1936, and what gas was used in airships after that date?

96. What was the name of the school teacher who was prosecuted for teaching the theory of evolution?

97. What is the more common name of Paralysis Agitans?

98. From which tree bark are the hand-made Japanese paper and Japanese vellum made?

99. Beri-Beri is caused by a deficiency in what vitamin?

100. What did Peter Heinlein build in 1502?

101. Which Monarch founded the Greenwich Observatory?

102. Who gave a 'Discourse on Light and Colour' to the Royal Society?

103. In 1988, the first US patent ever granted to a vertebrate (a mouse) was awarded. Why?

104. What are Adonis Blues, Commas, Dingy Skippers and Brimstones?

105. Muscardine is a disease that afflicts which creature?

106. The first travellers in a Montgolfier balloon were animals. One was a sheep, what were the others?

107. Which Parisian confectioner first succeeded in preserving foods in glass bottles?

108. Which process did Willard F Libby develop?

109. Who discovered the so-called Piltdown Man?

110. How large a percentage of the world's ice is contained in Antarctica?

111. In the USA around 1,000 human beings are bitten by snakes each year. How many of these result in death?

112. From 1872 to 1876, which British ship conducted the first major undersea survey?

113. Which creature has the Latin name *Carcharodon carcharias?*

114. What did Pierre and Paul-Jacques Curie discover in 1880?

115. Everyone knows that sailors were allowed a daily ration of limes and rum, but from 1823 all sailors were given one ounce per man per day of what?

116. Who made his way home from Rose Linda's and put himself on the road to a fortune?

117. Which everyday item was introduced to the United Kingdom in 1929 and soon saw off its cardboard rival?

118. Nicholas Kove introduced the first injection moulding machine into Britain; his company became world famous and is now part of Humbrol Limited. What is the name of the firm?

119. Which board game has sold over 60 million sets including versions in Russian and Greek?

120. In 1917, Count Callimachi invented something

he hoped would cure VD; it didn't but his invention is now in millions of households. What is it?

121. How long did the paddle steamer Savannah take to cross the Atlantic in 1819? (Allow 5 days either side.)

122. Which monarch decreed that no goldsmith was to sell a piece until it was assayed?

123. What is the standard mark for platinum?

124. How many toes does a bird have?

125. What species of bird is the most numerous in the USA?

126. Which tree is known by the Latin name of *Araucaria araucana* and an alternative name of Chile Pine?

127. What is the E number of monosodium glutamate?

128. Where would you find Mons Meg?

129. How long is the Mont Blanc Tunnel?

130. What is the name for the tough, straight-grained wood obtained from several different trees of the custard-apple family?

131. When did the lance make its final appearance on the battlefields of Europe?

132. What is glossolalia?

133. In what century did the practice of hallmarking gold and silver begin in the British Isles?

134. What is Pinchbeck made from?

135. What is measured on Moh's scale?

136. Which precious stone is made of calcium carbonate and calcium albuminate?

137. Which weed has the Latin name *Taraxacum officinale*?

138. Which scientist was born in Shrewsbury on February 12 1809 and died on April 19 1882?

139. What lies, for the most part, along the 180th meridian of longitude?

140. What name is given to a large upholstered sofa and a type of 18th century writing desk?

141. In chronological terms, what is a deadbeat?

142. What does a thanatologist study?

143. Who presents *The Sky at Night*?

144. What is psephology?

145. What is the decca system?

146. What was the name for the tin-glazed earthenware first made in 17th century Holland?

147. Where in the body is the deltoidus muscle?

148. What do demographers study?

149. What is dated by dendrochronology?

150. When Levi's jeans were first made, what fibre were they manufactured from?

151. What historic handshake took place between Graham Fagg and Phillipe Cozette on December 1 1990?

152. Apart from a dim character on an Australian soap opera, what is a drongo?

153. What piece of equipment used in the petroleum industry is named after a 17th century hangman?

154. What is a destroying angel?

155. In architecture, what is entablature?

156. What is another name for enteric fever?

157. What is an ephemeris?

158. What is the name for a unit of geological time during which a rock series is deposited?

159. Which precious stones are found in alluvial gravels, glacial tills and kimberlite pipes?

160. What is measured by an atmometer?

161. What type of submarine was Excalibur?

162. Which scientist defined man as 'the tool-making animal'?

163. In the shipping forecasts, which two area names are served by a Light Vessel Automatic?

164. Where in Britain is the National Railway Museum?

165. Who ran a temperance excursion on the Midland Counties Railway on July 5 1841?

166. Who was the builder of the first electric railway in Britain and the first person in Brighton to equip his house with a telephone and electric light?

167. North Americans call it a 'tie', the French call it 'la traverse', to the Germans it is 'die Schwelle'. What is it?

168. Under the Railways Act of 1921, railways were amalgamated into four groups. Name any two of them.

169. In radio, what do AM and FM stand for?

170. What is trepanning?

171. What does BTU stand for?

172. When did bubonic plague claim its last victim in the UK?

173. Which illness did Robert the Bruce die from?

174. What weighed 200 pounds and was discovered near Ballarat, Australia in 1869?

175. Which scientists refused to take out a patent on their process, declaring that the product belonged to the world and no one had any right to profit from it?

176. How long was Sir Christopher Wren's formal architectural training?

177. A smaller version of what was erected on one of the islands in the River Seine?

178. Which philanthropist worked as a millhand at the age of twelve and sold his own company fifty years later for 500 million dollars?

179. Name the element named after a human being.

180. Four elements are named after one Swedish town. Name any two of them.

181. What is the basic difference between organic and inorganic compounds?

182. Which well-known scientist devised a solution that saved the French silkworm industry?

183. How many pounds of coffee can be produced from the annual harvest of one coffee tree?

184. Which vegetable has been banned in different countries at different times for causing leprosy, rickets and for being an aphrodisiac?

185. How big is a nano-meter?

186. In the deadly London fog of December 1952, how many people died from ingesting the deadly fumes? (Allow two thousand either side.)

187. How many times was Newton elected as President of the Royal Society?

188. Who invented the aqualung?

189. What relation was Charles Darwin to Francis Galton, the first person to work out the use of fingerprints for identification?

190. Which Jesuit astronomer was the first to make colour drawings of Mars?

191. The hydrofoil boat belonging to a famous scientist set a world water speed record in 1919. Who was the scientist?

192. How tall are the smallest, naturally growing trees in the world?

193. What type of plane did Bryan Allen fly in June 1979?

194. Approximately how many years did Florence Nightingale spend nursing soldiers in the Crimea?

195. What is the melting point of the metal gallium?

196. Who produced the first fully automatic machine gun?

197. What does GATT stand for?

198. If you suffered from ailurophobia what would you be frightened of?

199. Who was the only US president to have a PhD degree?

200. Charles Messier devised a list of objects in the night sky that the serious comet hunter should avoid – he called one of these hazy objects Messier 31. Today it is much better known as which galaxy?

201. Which astronomer wore a false nose made of metal?

202. To within 10 billion, how many comets are estimated to be in the solar system?

203. What was the purpose of Project Osma?

204. Which common, mild disorder is also called epistaxis?

205. Who took out the first patent for a pneumatic tyre?

206. As what would a chickadee be known in Britain?

207. Which ornamental material was obtained from the hawksbill turtle?

208. Which famous agriculturalist wrote *The New Horse Houghing Husbandry*?

209. What is the name of a mechanical device that unites the threaded ends of two rods and permits them to be adjusted for length or tension?

210. In the human body, where would you find the utricle and saccule?

211. What element is named after the Scandinavian goddess of beauty and youth?

212. What medical procedure used to be known as variolation?

213. Where in the human body are von Ebner's glands?

214. What is the chemical symbol for tungsten?

215. What insect is also called the Cattle Grub or Heel Fly?

216. When did the Vatican absolve Galileo of the charges of heresy brought against him in 1633?

217. What is an arboretum?

218. What type of shape would you find in an item described as belemnoid?

219. What is another name for mercury sulphide?

220. What type of mineral is a citrine?

221. What is the name for areas of calm in equatorial waters?

222. What is the scientific name for a spider?

223. What is also known as Woolsorter's Disease?

224. How much fluid does a yard-of-ale glass hold?

225. What was the name of the hurricane that battered Florida in August 1992?

226. The liver of which animal was transplanted into a human subject in September 1992?

227. What make of car did the Princess of Wales give up after a storm of 'Buy British' protests?

228. Which car manufacturer produced its first new model for forty years in February 1993?

229. What is the name of the artificial stone used extensively during the 18th and 19th centuries?

230. What is parsec a contraction of?

231. How many tons does Big Ben weigh?

232. What is the oldest living thing?

233. Which breed of dog is descended from an Arabian greyhound and a Russian sheepdog?

234. What type of animal is a brocket?

235. What name of a type of carriage and a style of modern day car is derived from the french for 'leap'?

236. What is a *campanile*?

237. What is the term for a quadrilateral enclosure surrounded by covered walkways?

238. In which constellation would you find the dark nebula called the Coalsack?

239. What is the Genome project?

240. Generally speaking, dogs are colour-blind. For those breeds of dog which have limited colour vision, can you name one colour that they can distinguish?

241. Which pain-killer is derived from willow bark?

242. How did cosmonaut Yuri Gagarin die?

243. Approximately, what is the temperature of an oxyacetylene flame?

244. Which poison is also known as Wolfsbane or Monkshood?

245. What name was given to the Sikorsky S-42 flying boat?

246. Meteorologically speaking, what is a chinook?

247. At the summer solstice the sun is above the horizon for 16 hours and 38 minutes in London. If you are at the tip of Scotland, for how much longer would you see the sun above the horizon?

248. For a weather statistician, when does summer start and finish?

249. In which constellation is the star Aldebaran?

250. How is ambergris obtained?

251. What has variations called Mushroom, Danforth and Stockless?

252. Which London structure was demolished in the early sixties despite a massive protest and was recently found underwater?

253. What colour is the dye Annatto?

254. What type of animal is an anoa?

255. Which sweetener is marketed under the brand names NutraSweet and Canderel?

256. How many million gallons of mineral water were drunk in the UK in 1992?

257. Which Royal Society is situated at 1, Kensington Gore?

258. What is converted by multiplying by nine, dividing by five and adding thirty two?

259. What is the name for the quantity of heat required to raise the temperature of one gram of water by one degree centigrade?

260. Which word is used to describe metal that can be drawn out into wire or thread?

261. What was measured on the Reaumur Scale?

262. In physics, what is the term for a surface that absorbs all radiant energy falling on it?

263. In which century did the British military employ Congreve's Rocket?

264. What is the essential difference between a greenhouse and a conservatory?

265. What type of bird is a conure?

266. More than half the total world production of which precious stone is mined at the Australian site of Coober Pedy?

267. What is the name for a telescope which produces an artificial total eclipse of the sun?

268. What is the upper and lower limit on the number of people that make up a coroner's jury? (Allow an answer within five of each figure.)

269. Place the following in order of size: cruiser, destroyer, battleship.

270. What object appears on the flags of Western Samoa and New Zealand?

271. What name is given to the blue or purple discolouration of the skin which results from a deficiency of oxygen in the blood?

272. Who disappeared near Howland Island in the South Pacific in July 1937?

273. How many sides does a duodecagon have?

274. What is machicolation?

275. What plant produces saffron?

276. In the early days of railways, what was the measurement of broad-gauge railway tracks?

277. What is scagliola?

278. In what decade did the worst earthquake to hit Britain occur?

279. What does a Pirani gauge measure?

280. Which three elements were discovered in pitch-blende?

281. Which company registered 'Tabloid' as a trade mark?

282. Where were the first chip shops?

283. There are two reasons why mustard gas is a misnomer. What are they? (A point each.)

284. What was the lowest denomination note ever issued in Britain? (An extra point for the year of issue.)

285. Name an animal indigenous to the British Isles which hibernates?

286. Which common architectural feature takes its name from an early English name for a siege tower?

287. The fancy name for baldness is alopecia, but to which animal does this term refer?

288. In which year did London's first electric trams appear?

289. According to the World Tourism Organization, which country makes the most from tourism?

290. How many million cars were made world-wide in 1992?

291. In 1993, the first new large mammal to be discovered in 50 years was found in which country?

292. According to FAO, how many million tons of grain were shipped in Food Aid consignments during 1992–93?

293. In which shuttle did US astronauts travel to repair the Hubble Space Telescope?

294. According to the latest figures available to the World Drink Trends Survey, which country has the highest consumption of distilled spirits?

295. Which aeronautical project was refused further funding in 1988?

296. What is the minimum legal aging period for whisky?

297. Which oil gives Earl Grey tea its distinctive aroma?

298. Which fruit is also known as the Chinese Gooseberry?

299. What is the more common name of the English toy spaniel?

300. Which treelike desert plant, found in the south-western United States, is also known as the tree yucca, yucca palm or yucca cactus?

301. Which chemical was found in Perrier water and led the company to withdraw 160 million bottles from the world market?

302. Sheffield Plate was replaced by what new process?

303. Which item was made for the last time in 1813 and only issued to soldiers involved in the Peninsular Wars?

304. The amphora was an ancient Roman unit of capacity. Approximately how many gallons did it contain?

305. What is the name of the hybrid alpaca and llama bred specifically for its fleece?

306. What type of glassware takes its name from the Italian for 'thousand flowers'?

307. What type of animal is a midshipman?

308. What is another name for the marsh marigold?

309. What artificial human organ did Robert Jarvik invent?

310. What does CFC stand for?

311. What was the function of the satellite Tiros 1?

312. What is the name for a rapidly spinning neutron star that emits sharp bursts of electromagnetic energy?

313. What do the following products have in common: Brillo, Guinness, Shredded Wheat and Esso petrol?

314. Kansas City undertaker, Almon B Strowger, patented which modern development in March 1889? (Another two points if you know why he laboured so long to invent it.)

315. On September 26 1769, a lady with the unenviable name of Honoretta Tratt achieved posthumous fame. Why?

316. Carlton McGee, editor of the Oklahoma City Gazette, invented which demonic device in 1933?

317. Sir Samuel Peto, building contractor who erected Nelson's column, and Sir Henry Cole, father of the Christmas card, put their heads together to come up with Britain's first what?

318. Which British landmark is properly known as the Angel of Christian Charity?

319. What popular product in modern life was developed as a filter for gas masks?

320. Name the biggest herb on the planet.

321. Name the odd one out: peanut, hazelnut, walnut.

322. Name a popularly edible member of the thistle family.

323. Which gemstones hold the highest value, carat for carat?

324. Taking into consideration terms of trade, which really does weigh more – a ton of coal or a ton of feathers?

325. To equate a dog's age to human age you multiply the latter by a factor of seven. True or false?

326. As a rule how long does it take for alcohol to be processed through the body?

327. As a rule, how long does it take to completely digest a meal?

328. A cow needs three pounds of what to produce onc pound of milk?

329. The average person resting for one hour will burn how many calories?

330. In the cutting and polishing process of a diamond approximately what percentage of its weight is lost?

331. How much milk does it take to make a pound of cottage cheese?.

332. Who died in 1626 after contracting a severe

chill whilst conducting frozen food experiments by stuffing dead chickens with snow in his back garden at Highgate?

333. American comedian Bob Burns used a Heath Robinson type trumpet made from a length of stove-pipe. In the Second World War American troops gave Burns's nickname for this device to a weapon they used. What was it?

334. With the dawning of the age of Aquarius, what did Charles Prior Hall of California invent in 1970?

335. What is the name for a medical preparation or device that prevents or helps to prevent disease?

336. What was the name of the first unmanned space-ship to pass close to the moon?

337. In which decade was the first transatlantic telephone link between London and New York opened?

338. Which two archeologists discovered Tutan-khamen's tomb?

339. What nationality was Ernest Rutherford?

340. What is or was a prize court concerned with?

341. Over what period was Project Blue Book maintained?

342. What was the original occupation of J R Rank?

343. Which defect in vision is called protanopia?

344. Which colour used in heraldic design is called gules?

345. What is the name of the muscle which extends from the crest of the pelvic girdle down the front and side of the thigh and is attached to the inner and upper portion of the shin-bone?

346. Whereabouts is the Grand Hassan II Mosque and why does it use a laser beam?

347. Which car manufacturer opened its first Russian showroom in July 1993?

348. In 1993, scientists drilling through the ice cap in Greenland reached a record depth of 10,000 feet – they extracted an ice core deposited how many years ago?

349. Which writer was also a research fellow in entomology at Harvard University?

350. Which chocolate manufacturer created a model village called New Earswick?

351. Jean Dunant, Frederic Passy, Wilhelm Roentgen and Emil Von Behring: what do they have in common?

352. What was the name of the first British submarine?

353. When the Brownie camera went on sale in the US how much did it cost?

354. A concession to search for something was granted to William Knox D'Arcy in 1901. What was he searching for?

355. In 1901, wireless telegraphy at sea was tried for the first time. On which liner did the experiment take place?

356. What colour is the inside surface of a quail's egg?

357. The shipyards of which city produced the ill-fated Titanic?

358. In France, what percentage of the nation's electrical requirement is met by the nuclear industry?

359. What is a qurush?

360. Awarded the Nobel Prize in 1971, Dennis Gabor developed what?

361. By what name is the star Polaris more often known?

362. Where on the planet are the largest deposits of gold to be found?

363. When the Hubble telescope passes above in orbit how high up is it?

364. If you were rutilistic, how could people tell?

365. Lakes damaged by acid rain are treated to massive doses of what?

366. In which American state would you find the largest deposits of alabaster?

367. On an abacus, how many beads are there in each column?

368. Of all the known planets which is the largest?

369. Name the brightest star in the sky.

370. We all know Bikini Atoll was the site of the first atomic test in 1946. The island gradually repopulated but in what year did the US have to evacuate the new inhabitants when it was discovered that all plant and vegetable life on the island was cesium active?

371. What is Avogadro's number? (Not its value but what does it quantify?)

372. Learned settlers in America made great use of the pokeweed. Why?

373. Being quite specific, what is the largest organism on earth?

374. Walter Brattain was responsiblc for which technological breakthrough?

375. Which planet turned out to be composed almost entirely of methane?

376. What is made from the bark of the cinchona tree?

377. Sigmund Freud thought there were how many

main divisions of the human psyche? (One point for each one.)

378. Queen Victoria gave it to one son, two daughters and seven grandchildren. What was it?

379. Apart from water, what is the main ingredient of Coca-Cola?

380. Which heavenly body was first gazed upon by William Herschel?

381. By what other name is the constellation of The Great Bear known?

382. Herbert C Booth invented which machine of great wonderment in 1901?

383. What major astronomical discovery occurred in 1846?

384. At which part of the body is the skin found to be its thinnest?

385. By what term are the smallest blood vessels in the body known?

386. Name the smallest group of mammals.

387. Which nation was the first to achieve a crew-change in space?

388. The Emperor Nero used to watch gladiatorial games through a magnifying glass made from what?

389. Molinyia was the name the Russians gave to

a whole series of satellites launched in the late 1960s. What was the purpose of these satellites?

390. In the 1660s Anton van Leevwenhoek was the first man to see what, after plucking a piece of food from between his teeth?

391. The American Indian was called the redskin from a self-applied dye of that colour. Not only ceremonial paint, it was also an effective insecticide, but from what plant did they extract the dye?

392. Who invented the miners' safety fuse?

393. Which nation launched the weather satellite called Wind and Cloud Number One in 1988?

394. Air expelled from the nose during sneezing travels at approximately what speed?

395. Who perfected the milk-fat test in 1890, this now named in his honour?

396. In 1986 Lake Nyos in Cameroon disgorged massive quantities of a gas that killed some two thousand people and all livestock in the area. Name the gas.

397. Which of the senses is closest to the hippocampus?

398. In what year did the Eagle land on the moon?

399. Which fruit is most commonly used for the

stamping of clearance marks – date information etc – on meat?

400. How many stars are there in the constellation of Hydra?

401. In the binary system, 8 bits make up one what?

402. There is a gemstone nicknamed 'the queen of gems'. What is it?

403. In one year alone, two Viking probes landed on Mars. What was that year?

404. Who allegedly came up with 'I think, therefore I am'?

405. In the known skies how many constellations are there?

406. How many years does it take for Pluto to orbit the sun?

407. How long does it take for the body to produce a red blood cell?

408. John Dalton became the first scientist to define what?

409. What was the name of the first Russian spacecraft to become a permanently manned station in 1986?

410. What is the term for a number which will divide exactly into a given quantity?

411. The basic unit of the living organism is called what?

412. On average, how many tornadoes hit the United States every year?

413. According to Albert Einstein what game does God not play?

414. Who was the first astronomer to suggest that the sun – and not the earth – was the centre of the universe?

415. Which of the following planets is nearest to the sun: Mercury, Mars or Venus?

416. What is the largest organ of the human body?

417. In all, how many bones are there in the human skull?

418. Medieval beggars used a plant called cursed crowfoot to boost business. What did it produce for them to make them look even more pathetic?

419. Shaw's jird is less scientifically referred to as 'the big bang mouse'. Why?

420. The star-nosed mole is so named for the numerous projections on its hooter – but how many are there?

421. The Northern Grasshopper mouse enjoys a dangerous diet. What is it?

422. What is the largest artery in the human body?

423. Which scientist played the key role in producing

the first atomic bomb? (Extra point for the code name of his project.)

424. In 1983 an artificial sweetener was finally approved for use in soft drinks. What was it?

425. Which part of the body did nearly all ancient cultures believe to be the seat of intelligence?

426. How tall is the statue of Nelson on Nelson's Column?

427. The founder and editor of the Wall Street Journal made another enduring contribution to the understanding of money and commodity markets. What is it?

428. The two German astronomers who actually discovered Neptune were told where to look by a French astronomer – he lost the battle to have the planet named after him. Who was he?

429. Which two companies merged to form General Motors?

430. When did Coca-Cola go on sale in Britain?

431. What was the name of America's first female astronaut?

432. When the Model T Ford ceased production which model took its place?

433. Over which state did the Hindenberg explode?

434. How many months did the Festival of Britain last?

435. Wren had another church in mind when he modelled the dome of St Paul's. Which church was it?

436. Who opened a '5 and 10 Cent Store' in Pennsylvania?

437. For what purpose was the Alcor Corporation established?

438. Approximately how many doctors per year take the Hippocratic Oath in the United Kingdom alone?

439. At how many millimetres per month does human hair grow?

440. The deadly poison bufotoxin is extracted from which creature?

441. An American company translated their world-famous slogan, in order to enter the Far Eastern markets, only to inform the prospective purchaser that they could 'bring their ancestors back to life'. With what?

442. By what name is Ignis Fatuus better known?

443. Which two nuts are mentioned in the Bible? (One point each.)

444. Which particular acid was first identified from a substance found in the thorax of the ant?

445. The word 'robot' was taken from the Czech language. What does it mean?

446. Which creatures have spent more time in space than any other?

447. Sylvan Goldman, grocery store owner in Oklahoma, USA, invented what?

448. A dog named Stanley belonging to ex-pats living in Spain became the first canine to wear what?

449. Which popular product is known to its manufacturers as Merchandise 7X?

450. An American company called Symbol hold patent on many aspects of what modern development?

451. Which nation first developed paper money?

452. In the first demonstration of the telephone, Bell summoned his assistant from a separate room with what instruction?

453. Some four poster beds have a canopy extending only half the length of the mattress. What is such a bed called?

454. A certain biological structure finds itself devoid of blood upon death; it achieved its modern name because ancient anatomists thus thought its purpose was the channelling of air. What is it?

455. What style of boat is named from the German verb meaning 'to hunt'?

456. Who coined the expression 'animal magnetism'?

457. Which country has the largest population of wild camels?

458. What are American astronauts not allowed to eat for forty-eight hours before take off?

459. Name the closest star to the earth.

460. In the 1930s vicuna coats were very popular but where does vicuna come from?

461. How many teats per udder has a Jersey cow?

462. A common architectural feature of vaulted roofs in cathedrals and the like is named for its resemblance of two goats reared up with horns locked. What is it?

463. Which North American marsupial is believed to play dead?

464. On Lloyd's Shipping Register, A 1 indicates a ship in perfect condition. The letters and numbers signify two different categories, what are they? (A point each.)

465. In 1937 Croydon was hit by an epidemic causing forty-three deaths. What was the disease?

466. What cannot fall when the ground temperature is below zero?

467. In what year was the first high-seas lighthouse completed? (One point for year, one for location.)

468. Prior to 1972, what was the name of the airworthiness authority of the UK?

469. In 1902 Ronald Ross received the Nobel Prize for his work in combatting which disease?

470. In what year was the Automobile Association founded?

471. In 1865 the Road Locomotion Act was passed, what speed limit was imposed and how many attendants were required for each moving vehicle?

472. What was seen for the first time in a long time on October 11 1982?

473. In 1801, Dalton's Law regarding pressure in gasses was first formulated. By whom?

474. In which year was the Royal College of Physicians founded in London?

475. In 1589 a clergyman of Nottinghamshire called William Lee invented what?

476. In which year did the city of London receive its first pumped water supplies?

477. In 1703 large quantities of a strange new substance were found in the holds of three captured Spanish ships. A finely ground brown dust it was soon all the rage at the London court. What was it?

478. In which year did Sir Clive Sinclair's doomed C5 go on sale?

479. In 1979, Geoffrey Hounsfield received the Nobel

Prize for medicine for his invention of the computerised axial tomographic body scanner. By what name is it better known?

480. Where in the human body would you find the antrum of Highmore?

481. In geology, what is the name for a rock formation containing water in recoverable quantities?

482. In electrical enginieering what does BDV stand for?

483. What is deglutition?

484. In botany, if something is described as flabelliform what shape is it?

485. Mimas is the natural satellite orbiting closest to which planet?

486. What is a mimetic diagram?

487. What is a parasheet?

488. What programme did Professor Heinz Wolff devise and present during the 1980s on BBC2?

489. What fashion development first appeared in 1965 and was popularised by Mary Quant?

490. In 1959 Californian entrepreneur Ruth Handler and her designer husband launched a new toy on the market. What was it?

491. In 1958 Whamm-O manufacturing in America sold 100 million what?

492. In October 1829 the Rainhill Speed Trials were held near Liverpool. Who and what won the day?

493. Who set sail, on perhaps the most significant voyage in the annals of science, on December 22 1831?

494. On October 3 1896 William Downey took the first moving film of any Royals. Featured, of course, was Queen Victoria and another Royal family. One point to identify the family group and another for the location.

495. Which major freight route was opened by Queen Victoria on the May 21 1894?

496. After being jammed on the slipway for ten weeks which ship was finally launched at Millwall on January 31 1858?

497. In February 1855 who patented a process for converting pig iron into steel?

498. In what year did the mixamatosis epidemic hit Britain and where did it come from? (One point each.)

499. Who discovered X-Rays?

500. Which major new toy craze was launched in America in 1902 and after whom was it named?

501. The British Royal family suddenly felt the need for

twenty-seven diamond tiaras to be perched on the heads of assorted female hangers-on attending the coronation of Edward VII. As ever the order went out of the country to a French jeweller. What was his name?

502. Many reptiles are mute. Which two have the loudest voices?

503. By what name is a *hummum* better known in Britain?

504. Cutaneous diseases affect which part of the body?

505. By what more whimsical name is the Russian vine better known?

506. What is the gestation period of the ass?

507. Emperor Menelik II of Abyssinia used which device as his imperial throne?

508. Venus is known by a perhaps more poetic name. What is it?

509. In Britain, how many boys are born for every hundred girls?

510. For much of its length, the A5 is laid over which old Roman road?

511. France perhaps has the greatest variety of cheese but which country has the greatest variety of sausage?

512. What are the two main ingredients of Cock-a-leekie soup?

513. Who was the first British royal to take to the highways in an automobile?

514. The poult is the young of which bird?

515. In what year did Concorde first fly the Atlantic?

516. Which part of the body is the most sensitive to radiation?

517. What do somatologists study?

518. To which creature does the collective noun 'smuck' apply?

519. The average human scalp sheds how many hairs a day?

520. Which English assay city is identified by a rose?

521. How many squares in a Rubik cube never shift position?

522. Louis Washkansky became famous for eighteen days. Why?

523. The first television sets in Britain showed a picture made up of how many lines?

524. By what name is the Kookaburra otherwise known?

525. The milk of which creature is pink?

526. What is measured by an interferometer?

527. What distinction is peculiar to osmium?

528. Who was Richard Branson's partner during his transatlantic balloon flight?

529. What meteorological phenomenon takes its name from the Arabic for a season?

530. What animals collect in a clowder?

531. How long did it take the Voyager space probe to reach Neptune?

532. Which country first got its flag to the moon?

533. If you suffered from anosmia how would you be deficient?

534. In a square kilometre of sea water, how many tons of salt are there?

535. What type of device was that which was nicknamed a Marconi box?

536. What is the next word in this sequence: Viking, Forties, Cromarty, Forth and . . .?

537. Everybody knows what an isobar joins but what is joined by an isonet?

538. Where is the longest mountain range on earth and what is its name? (One point each.)

539. How do frogs breathe underwater?

540. Name a food substance which is in turn named after a snake?

541. What do Gazpacho and Vichyssoise have in common?

542. The axis of the earth is continually shifting and, in about ten thousand years, it is estimated that the Pole Star as a bearing reference will be replaced by which other star?

543. If you bought a can of Mace, what type of gas would be in it?

544. What do all native Australian flowers lack?

545. There are countless satellites which orbit the earth. Name the largest.

546. On the last day of her life, Marie Curie became the first person to do what?

547. The bathypelagic zone in the sea starts at one thousand metres and goes down how much further?

548. What is the collective term for salmon?

549. There are seven regions of the UK legally allowed to issue postage stamps. (One point each for any five.)

550. By how much does the level of the sea drop in spring?

SPORT AND LEISURE

1. How old was Dr W G Grace when he retired from playing cricket?
2. Which Canadian sportsman's world ranking fell from 4th place in 1985 to 78th place in 1989?
3. Of which sportsman did a physiotherapist say: 'He's incredibly loyal. Ask him to jump off the stand roof and he'd do it but he's as thick as two short planks'?
4. Which writer was disqualified after winning the 1868 Civil Service Five Mile Walk Championships?
5. Name any three of the nine counties who contested the first cricket County Championships.
6. Who gave Henry VIII a set of darts as a present?

7. Which rugby player threw a bed out of a hotel window in Pretoria during a bout of post match frivolity?
8. In the Los Angeles Olympic Women's 3,000 metres final, which two athletes collided?
9. Still with that much discussed final, who actually won the race?
10. In 1977 Virginia Wade won the Ladies' Singles competition at Wimbledon, who was her opponent?
11. What sport was the subject of the film *This Sporting Life*?
12. Who was the first woman to hit a six in a Test Match at Lord's?
13. Which rider told camera-men in 1973: 'You camera-men are getting my goat. Horses are very sensitive . . . they don't understand what all the fuss is about'?
14. Where is the world's largest race-course?
15. Who said of himself: 'I've got a bad swing, a bad stance and a bad grip. But my banker loves me'?
16. What was the name of the Suffragette who threw herself in front of the King's horse?
17. Which sportsman was nicknamed the 'Ebony Antelope'?

18. Under what name was Manchester United known before 1902?

19. Which football club has the nickname 'The Merry Millers'?

20. What is the legal limit of letters in a race horse's name?

21. In which decade did Rugby League reduce the number of players in a team from fifteen down to thirteen?

22. Which Conservative chancellor introduced the betting tax in 1926?

23. Which boxer said, in 1987. 'I want to become the Michael Caine of the nineties', when he was offered a part in a film?

24. Which football club had the first all-seated stadium in the British Isles?

25. When Paul Gascoigne transferred from Tottenham to Lazio, what was the fee?

26. 1979 saw three £1 million transfers between British clubs, name any one of the players involved.

27. Who won the women's competition in the London Marathon in 1984, 85, 87 and 88?

28. Who is the only person to win the BBC Sports Personality of the Year award twice?

29. What is the name of the award made annually to the American sportsman or woman who has contributed most to good sportsmanship?

30. In what decade was the World Badminton Championship launched?

31. Which city has staged the most world heavyweight title fights?

32. In pounds or kilograms, what is the weight limit for a boxer in the straw-weight or mini-flyweight division?

33. Which country has taken the most Olympic boxing medals?

34. On which stand at Lord's cricket ground is Father Time situated?

35. Who is the only woman to appear in the obituaries of cricketers in *Wisden's Almanack*?

36. Which is the oldest golfing club in Britain?

37. Where has the Greyhound Derby been held since 1984?

38. Which two of the five British Classic horse races are held over a distance of 1 mile and 4 furlongs?

39. In which sport is the Hart Trophy awarded?

40. Which female tennis player has won the most Grand Slam tennis titles?

41. In 1980, Bjorn Borg won his fifth and final Wimbledon singles title, who was his opponent?

42. When was tennis discontinued as an Olympic Event?

43. According to the Office of Populations, Censuses and Surveys, what is the most popular participation sport for men in the UK?

44. According to Ladbrokes, what is the sporting event to attract most betting?

45. Which motorcyclist has the most Grand Prix race wins?

46. Which motor-cycle manufacturer has the most Grand Prix wins?

47. Which car manufacturer was the first to win 100 Grands Prix?

48. Who holds the record for Olympic medals won at one celebration?

49. What sport boasts the oldest continuous world championship?

50. In the 1991/92 snooker season, who was the top money-winner?

51. In 1987 Alex Higgins was fined £12,000 for what offence?

52. Who scored the first maximum break in the history of the World Professional Championship?

53. Which squash player has the most wins in the British Open?

54. What combination of events make up the triathlon?

55. Which game was invented in 1895 and called Mintonette?

56. Which sport was included in the Olympics from 1900 to 1920?

57. In which year was the first women's World Snooker Championship held?

58. What are the three main weapons used in fencing?

59. What did Mercedes Gleitz achieve in 1927?

60. In which decade did the *News of the World* Darts Championships begin?

61. When does the Icelandic soccer season begin?

62. How many times did Red Rum run in the Grand National?

63. Who was the first jockey to be knighted?

64. How many players are there in an Australian Rules Football team?

65. Who is generally, but erroneously, credited with the invention of baseball?

66. Who competes for the Curtis Cup?

67. What is the national summer game of Canada?

68. In the English Club Lacrosse Championships, which club has amassed the most wins?

69. Name all the events in the modern pentathlon.

70. How many pieces does each player have in backgammon?

71. For which game did Harold Vanderbilt devise a scoring table?

72. Which Rugby Union trophy competition was played from 1966 to 1980?

73. Which football club became a limited company on June 1 1982?

74. Why did Stockport County consider changing the colours of their strip in 1982?

75. Which was the first Football League club to install an artificial pitch?

76. In which decade was Wimbledon first televised?

77. Which city has the oldest racecourse in continuous use?

78. Who is the only Grand Prix driver to have won the World Championship posthumously?

79. When did the Isle of Man T T races begin?

80. Who was the trainer of Grand National winner Corbière?

81. At which Olympic games were the five rings of the Olympic flag first seen?

82. What is the permitted width of a cricket bat?

83. Which two sports were added to the 1992 Olympics?

84. How many sports (not counting demonstration events) are represented at the Olympics?

85. Name either of the British rowers who won the Coxless Pairs gold medal at the Barcelona Olympics?

86. How are bows in archery competitions rated?

87. For what sporting action did Britons Ivan Lawler and Graham Burns win the International Fair Play Award in 1991?

88. In what decade was the Sports Council established?

89. When were the last tandem races seen in the Olympic games?

90. Of the current Olympic events, name two where men and women compete together.

91. Name any two events in the pentathlon of ancient times.

92. In the Olympic tennis event, what is the playing surface?

93. What did the referee in the 1966 FA Cup Final get that none of his predecessors had?

94. Which boxing term, now in general use, describes fighting at such close quarters that no proper punches can be thrown?

95. How many Premiership points for the 1994/95 season did Tottenham Hotspur have deducted by the FA for financial irregularities?

96. Which extremely successful boxer earned over $4.5 million during his career, yet retired with nothing in the bank and a tax bill of $1 million?

97. Which boxer of the 19th century had the nick-name Kid McCoy?

98. Which actor was scheduled to play Rocky Graziano in the film *Somebody Up There Likes Me* but was replaced by Paul Newman?

99. Where was Joe Bugner born?

100. Which boxer, later a millionaire MP, was portrayed by Dickens as Mr Gregsbury in Nicholas Nickleby?

101. Which was the first country to issue stamps depicting boxers?

102. How old was George Foreman when he challenged Evander Holyfield in 1991?

103. Against whom did Muhammed Ali have his last fight before retiring?

104. In their first match of the 1994 World Cup, which team was defeated by Ireland?

105. Why did Brough Scott, Lord Oaksey and Oliver Sherwood run in the 1983 London Marathon?

106. Why are The Byerley Turk, The Godolphin Arabian and The Darley Arabian so important to modern day racing?

107. What is the official birthday for all horses?

108. Who was the first woman to complete the Grand National course?

109. What sport did Sir Arthur Conan Doyle and George Bernard Shaw practise?

110. How long is a regulation cricket bat?

111. What is the weight of a cricket ball?

112. In *Wisden's Almanack*, what is the only animal to have been mentioned in the obituaries?

113. What is the term for a cricket ball that moves in flight from off to leg?

114. What term do the Australians use for a groundsman?

115. What type of race is the Iditarod?

116. How many times has Eddie Merckx won the Tour de France?

117. Approximately how many miles/kilometres are covered in the Tour De France?

118. In what year did Nigel Mansell win the Formula One World Championship?

119. How old was Nigel Short when he became a chess grand master?

120. Under what age do you not require a national rod fishing licence?

121. Apart from the obvious tag, how can fishermen recognise salmon or sea trout that have been tagged by the National River Authority?

122. In the world of angling, what is a fighting chair?

123. In what year was the maximum wage limit for professional footballers abandoned?

124. Which football league club was the first to become a limited company?

125. How many times did Alex Stepney play for Chelsea before being sold to Manchester United?

126. How many footballers died in the 1958 Munich air disaster?

127. In a tennis match, the score is deuce; one player goes on to win the game. How many points have been scored in total by both players?

128. Which player defeated Steffi Graf in the first round of the 1994 Wimbledon championships?

129. What is the full name of the club which organises the Wimbledon tennis championships?

130. How many Marquess of Queensberry rules are there?

131. Which tennis player married and became Mrs Norman Brinker?

132. Left unemployed by The Great Depression, Alfred Butts sat at home to devise a board that he patented in 1948. What name did he register?

133. Laurel leaves were given to athletes at which Greek games?

134. What make of car was Jim Clark driving when he was killed?

135. In which year did both boats in the Oxford and Cambridge Boat Race sink?

136. In which year were the Wimbledon championships opened to professional players?

137. Which US city hosts the Preakness Stakes?

138. Why was Muhammed Ali disqualified from boxing during the late 1960s?

139. In golf, what is a stymie?

140. Which British footballer joined Italian club Bari for a fee of £6 million?

141. When Kenny Dalgleish quit his job as manager at Liverpool, what reason was given?

142. Which three Scottish League clubs have compass points in their names?

143. Tottenham's fine for making irregular payments to its players was increased in July 1994 from £600,000 to what? How many of the previously imposed penalty points were removed?

144. In the 1994 Lausanne Grand Prix which athlete ran the fastest ever 100 metres race?

145. Who were the male and female champions of Wimbledon in 1994?

146. Which rugby side took the Calcutta Cup in February 1991?

147. In which century was the first book on swimming published?

148. Where was Monica Seles playing tennis when she was stabbed?

149. During the 1992 Olympic Games, how many new world swimming records were set?

150. In which sport did Black Bears compete against Ellerston White?

151. Name any two of the major English horse races won by Opera House in 1993?

152. In the 1993 World (Track) Cycling Championships how many different events could male entrants compete for?

153. Which country became the ninth Test-playing nation?

154. In which game do players compete for the Bermuda Bowl?

155. Nigel Short and Gary Kasparov battled their way through the unofficial World Chess Championships. Who were the two players contesting the official World Championships at the same time?

156. In 1993, which boxer was crowned WBC heavyweight champion without having to put on his boxing gloves?

157. Which incident disrupted the Riddick Bowe v Evander Holyfield boxing match in Las Vegas, 1993?

158. In 1993 who became the youngest winner ever of a world-ranking snooker tournament?

159. In which sport did Willie Mosconi achieve fifteen world championship titles?

160. What make of car did Nigel Mansell drive in his first season of Indy-Car Competition?

161. In the 1993 Italian Grand Prix, what was the average speed of Damon Hill's car?

162. World championships in which sport were held at Borlange in Sweden during June 1993?

163. What was the *Earthwinds Hilton*?

164. In 1993 Victoria Van Meter became the youngest person ever to fly across the US from east to west. How old was she?

165. Which famous cricketer also won the South Australian Squash championship?

166. Which sport has a goal that is eight feet wide and six feet high?

167. According to the *Sporting Times*, what died on August 29 1882?

168. What is the name for the four players who comprise a curling team?

169. Why does the world of horse racing owe a debt of gratitude to the son of an Archbishop and Primate of New Zealand?

170. Which sport was enjoyed by the late Shah of Persia, Pundit Nehru, King Farouk and the young Princess (now Queen) Elizabeth?

171. In which year did Jackie Stewart, Graham Hill and John Surtees come first, second and third in the US Grand Prix?

172. During which World Cup '90 match did Paul Gascoigne burst into tears after being booked?

173. In the 1990 World Cup, which team defeated Argentina in the opening match?

174. What was the name of the yacht captained by Tracy Edwards and an all woman crew which took part in the Whitbread Round the World Race?

175. What is the real first name of basketball player 'Magic' Johnson?

176. Who did Martina Navratilova compete against in the final of Wimbledon 1990, a match which brought her a record ninth title?

177. Which former sportsman and commentator donned a turquoise tracksuit during 1991?

178. Which ancient sport was won when one participant struck the wall of a church with his riding crop?

179. The goal in lacrosse is how many feet square?

180. Which sport involves granite stones weighing approximately 44 pounds each?

181. In what year was the American National Ten Pin Bowling League set up?

182. Which piece of sporting equipment can either be single, side by side or over and under?

183. There are three main categories of ski-ing style. One is free style, which basically means do what you want; what are the other two?

184. In the Highland games there is much tossing of the caber. How long is the caber and what tree is it made from? (One point each.)

185. Which sport takes place in the Salle D'Armes?

186. What is the maximum number of dogs allowed to compete in an American greyhound race?

187. Which essential piece of sports equipment ranges in length from 0.9 of a metre to 2.4 metres long but can be no wider than 0.9 of a metre irrespective of its length?

188. Which all-round competition includes an event called bulldogging?

189. Which sport relies on sculls?

190. Which activity emerged as an international sport in 1951 when adherents met in Yugoslavia for the first world championships?

191. Which major field sport went into decline in the 17th century when longbows became more easily handled and accurate over a short range?

192. In which sport is the quarrel an essential piece of equipment?

193. In 1742, in the state of Virginia, which particular blood sport was instituted by the Colonial Governor?

194. In which century did mountain climbing become a recognised sport/pastime and which major peak was successfully scaled to make it so? (One point each.)

195. Which Japanese sport involves fencing with bamboo swords?

196. Which two sports were derived from Jujitsu during the last century?

197. Of which particular sport is 'Catch as Catch Can' an accepted style?

198. Which British sporting champion appeared in a film called *Space Riders* (1985)?

199. Which heavyweight boxing champion appeared in a feature film called *The Spirit of Youth*?

200. In which Bond film did tennis player Viraj Amritraj make an appearance?

201. In the 1920s, which pouting starlet was supposed to have slept with the entire University of Southern California in the one night?

202. Which famous comedy actor, now dead, was at one time the vice-president of the London Judo Society?

203. Which one time Italian featherweight boxing champion starred in *South Pacific*? A further point for the title of a film, very close to his

home country, in which he was killed in the opening sequence.

204. Which American soap actor was a baseball radio commentator for many years?

205. Katharine Hepburn was, in her teens, the gold medal champion in the State of Connecticut for which sport?

206. A popular term for the final conclusion is derived from the sport of archery where this word described the highest scoring arrow in the contest. What was the word?

207. Which game, named after a type of mask, was introduced to Britain by French prisoners held in this country during the Napoleonic Wars?

208. How did the American quarter-horse get its name?

209. In the game of Scrabble, if you placed the **X** on a double letter score square, what would be the total number of points for that letter?

210. In the game of Trivial Pursuit, what is the colour for sports and leisure questions?

211. Which game was invented in the late 19th century by bored British officers on service in India?

212. Many early ball games were played with the flat

of the open hand – as indeed some still are, e.g. Fives and the Eton Wall Game – but the old Arabic term for the palm of the hand is alive and well in British sporting terminology. What is that word?

213. Apart from lawn tennis, there is of course Real Tennis, but what does Real actually mean?

214. Which pub game gave us the expressions 'To turn the corner' and 'not in the same street'?

215. In medieval England you could be disembowelled for owning which type of dog?

216. Which famous actor, large for his age at fourteen, used to beat up the kid next door? That kid later fought as Rocky Marciano?

217. We've all heard the sporting expression 'We wuz robbed', but who said it and after which contest?

218. Which American Olympic swimming champion made it into the movies opposite Jane?

219. Many sports feature in films as the background to the plot. One point for the sport most often used and one point for the sport least often used.

220. Which famous American actor was, quite appropriately, America's small bore target shooting champion three times running?

221. Which popular fairground ride is a hand-me-down from knights training for the joust?

222. There is a much played game in Britain based on a rather vicious game once played by the American Indians. By what name is it known?

223. What was the name of the famous banked motor-racing track of England?

224. In English phraseology, 'to knuckle under' means 'to give in'. From which still popular pub game does this derive?

225. In the sport of Tug-of-War, what is the traditional and numerical command for the teams to take up the strain?

226. In martial arts grades of proficiency are denoted by the term *dan*. What does this mean in Japanese?

227. The London district of Soho takes its name from the hunting cry of which sport?

228. In a hurling match, play is divided into two halves. How long is each half?

229. What is the difference between the shortest hurdles race for men and women – in distance that is?

230. An equal result in a sporting contest is called a draw but this is a shortening of another term. What is it?

231. The Epsom Grand Metropolitan Stakes (sponsored by those who produce steaks of a different kind), is run over what distance?

232. Which lady jockey was to be found serving behind a counter in Harrods in 1987?

233. In 1969 Rodney Marsh of Queen's Park Rangers was awarded a disability pension of £1.35. Why?

234. In 1968 the boxing authorities invited Joe Frazier, Floyd Patterson and six others to slug it out between them for the heavyweight title. Why?

235. Who rode a home-made bicycle that used washing machine bearings, to break a world record in Hamar, Norway?

236. Which two American football teams staged an exhibition match in London in August 1993?

237. In which country did Chris Boardman break the world record for one-hour cycling – he covered 32.48 miles?

238. Two distinct reference marks are used when timing transatlantic races – one point for each.

239. What was allowed at the 1993 Royal Regatta that hadn't been allowed in the 154 previous events?

240. What was the only Grand Slam tennis title to elude Bjorn Borg?

241. James Fixx was the man who was said to have turned America on to what sport?

242. Who was the manager of Scotland's 1978 World Cup team?

243. In 1978, who was the first boxer to beat Muhammed Ali for the World Heavyweight boxing title?

244. In which year did Bjorn Borg win the last of his five Wimbledon singles titles?

245. Which gymnast was awarded the first perfect 10.00 in the history of the Olympics?

246. Which British swimmer won the gold medal for 200m breaststroke in the Montreal Olympics?

247. Which Minister for Sport also became Minister for Drought in 1976?

248. Which athlete was nicknamed 'The Flying Finn'?

249. What caused the August 1975 Cricket Test Match to be abandoned?

250. In 1974 who defeated Jorge Ahumada to become Britain's first holder of the World light-heavy-weight title in twenty-five years?

251. Which golfer won the 1994 British Open at Turnberry?

252. In 1973 many of the top players refused to play at Wimbledon. Who won the men's final?

253. How long is an ice hockey playing area?

254. Which motor-racing category restricts competitors to two-litre, four-cylinder production engines?

255. What nickname was given to Jack Brabham?

256. An unexpected change in the weather from a Force 8 to a Force 10 gale created a tragic and chaotic ending to which 1979 sporting event?

257. When Chay Blyth sailed round the world in 1971 what was the name of the vessel he used?

258. In the first ever football World Cup which two teams contested the final?

259. In which year was football's Women's World Cup first played and which team won?

260. On May 25 1935, how many world records did Jesse Owens set?

261. Where in Oxford was the athletics track where Roger Bannister ran the sub four-minute mile?

262. Still with Roger Bannister's historic run, how many other athletes took part in that same race?

263. From the time she signed the application, how long did Zola Budd have to wait for British citizenship to be granted?

264. In which male dominated sport did Davina Galica and Giovanna Amati compete?

265. What was the name for the mass gymnastic display which took place in Strahov Stadium, Prague

before the dismantling of the Communist Bloc?

266. 7, 16, 8: what is the next number in this sequence?

267. Which pastime is presided over by the ETWA?

268. Which ex-snooker champion brought Hurricane Higgins over from Ireland?

269. During the 1980s, how many times did Steve Davis meet Joe Johnson in the World Championship final?

270. Which sport were the crowd watching when they saw the Bulldog defeat the Plumb?

271. Which boxer was known as the Shambling Alp?

272. How long is the waiting list to join the world famous golf club at St Andrews?

273. In 1759, Belgian violin maker Joseph Merlin invented which piece of sporting equipment to cut a dash at a fancy dress ball?

274. An ancient Phillipino weapon of war is now a popular child's toy/pastime. What is its name?

275. In what year was the first formal yacht race which promoted such activity as a recognised sport?

276. In what year was the Ascot Gold Cup first run?

277. In 1618 an edict of King James I decreed as outlawful which genteel pastime?

278. Which established part of English folk culture was outlawed in 1647 by Cromwell's new administration?

279. In 1711 Queen Anne oversaw the layout of which great sporting facility?

280. In 1754 the first codified rules were drawn up for which sport?

281. These rules were codified by John Graeme Chambers in 1867. By what name are the rules better known?

282. Which famous sporting club was founded by a group of enthusiasts at the Star and Garter Coffee House in London's Pall Mall?

283. What type of sporting event ws first held in 1868 in the Parc De Saint Cloud in Paris?

284. What major change affected the football league after relaxation of certain legislation in 1981?

285. Which card game was introduced to Queen Victoria in 1871, at a royal party in Somerset, by the ambassador of a certain country famously associated with that very game?

286. Who did Buster Douglas knock out in Tokyo to take the world heavyweight crown in 1990?

287. In 1986 who romped home to win the Kentucky Derby at the age of fifty-four and bankrupted a few bookies by doing it on a 17–1 outsider?

288. In 1744 the country of Kent pitted its best against an all-England team in the first recorded contest of which sport?

289. Which famous horse-race was instituted in 1779?

290. Which club was founded in 1787 specifically to codify the rules of cricket?

291. Where did Steve Cram set the new mile record at 3.46 minutes in 1985?

292. To whom did Anatoly Karpov lose his world master title in Tchaikovsky's concert hall, Moscow in 1985?

293. *Freedom* defeated Australia by 4–1 to take which cup?

294. In which decade did the first gambling casino open in Monte Carlo?

295. Association Football or soccer, was instituted by the Football Association in which year?

296. In the 1976 Olympics, Soviet athletes really topped the bill. How many gold medals did they win in all?

297. In which year and where, did George Foreman take the world heavyweight title from Joe Frazier? (One point for year, one point for location.)

298. In which country was the first car road race

staged and in which year was it? (One point for each.)

299. Who set up the first annual motor racing cup in 1900?

300. Which new sport was invented in 1891 by Professor James Naismith of the Massachusetts YMCA, after serious rain had knocked out all planned sporting events?

301. The Marxburger Guild of Lowenburg in Germany set up the first association for which sporting activity in 1383?

302. The television series entitled *The Power and the Glory* was about which sport?

303. Which snooker player presented the series *Play Snooker*?

304. When the *Radio Times* printed a picture of a football pitch so that radio listeners could follow the match commentary, how many squares was it divided into?

305. When were the first Pan-American games scheduled to start and when did they actually begin?

306. Where were the 1972 Winter Olympics held?

307. In which Olympic event did Andre Agassi's father compete?

308. In which century were the first books on billiard playing techniques published?

309. America's *Rule and Record Book* for pool gives rules for how many variations on pool?

310. In badminton how high is the centre of the net from the ground?

311. On a standard table tennis table, how far will the ball rebound if dropped on the surface?

312. How many member nations are there in the International Table Tennis Federation?

313. How many points must one side amass to win a volleyball game?

314. What is the name of the version of racquetball for three players?

315. How many players are there in a Gaelic Football team?

316. Roque is a US version of which game?

317. How long is a polo pitch?

318. Professional basketball games are divided into quarters. How many minutes in each quarter?

319. How many cards are dealt to Baccarat players?

320. In the card game Ecarte how many cards are removed from the pack before dealing begins?

321. How many pieces are there in a set of dominoes?

322. In a chess game the board is placed so that the corner square to the right of each player is which colour?

323. In Mah Jongg each player has to build a wall out of their tiles. How many tiles long is it?

324. Which modern game is based on the old English game of hazard?

325. How many points must be scored to win a game of cribbage?

326. How many yards long is a standard golf course?

327. What is John McEnroe's middle name?

328. Everyone has heard of the historic 112 game match of Pancho Gonzales and Charlie Pasarell at Wimbledon, but what is Pancho's real first name?

329. How many players in a Canadian football team?

330. Who is the oldest tennis player ever to beat a number one ranked player?

331. How many numbered compartments are there on a roulette wheel?

332. If a betting shop refused to pay winnings what could the hapless punters legally do about it?

333. Who was the first person to ban hunting during animal breeding seasons?

334. The wood of which fruit tree is often used for the heads of golf clubs?

335. Which three horse races comprise the Triple Crown?

336. In the Luge events, how fast can the luge move?

337. About how long is a dog racing track?

338. In an international diving competition what is the maximum height for a springboard?

339. In which European city are the headquarters of the International Olympic Committee?

340. How many scheduled Olympic Games have been cancelled because of war?

341. How many countries withdrew from the 1980 Olympics?

342. Which sporting activity makes the most use of the body's muscles?

343. How many different types of yachting events were contested at the Olympics in 1988?

344. A kayak is only used by a male Inuit, what is the name for the boat used by the female Inuit?

345. How many types of competition are contested on roller-skates?

346. What is the name of the international governing body of tennis?

347. A splitter is the name given to the ball in which sport?

348. Friedrich Ludwig Jahn is regarded as the father of which sport?

349. On a pommel horse how far apart are the handles?

350. What sport was born in 1921 on Lake D'Annecy?

351. In 1936 American engineer George Nissen built the first Model T for the sporting world. What was it?

352. In 1874 a certain game was patented as Sphairistike by Captain Walter Wingfield. By what name is this game better known today?

353. Which horse-race was first run at Louisville's Churchill Downs Course in 1875?

354. In 1973, American tennis player Bobby Riggs boasted that no woman could beat him over five sets. Which woman did at the Houston Astrodome?

355. In what year did Tony Jacklin become the first Briton to win the US Open in fifty years?

356. What was the Louisville Slugger?

357. Which American baseball team's home ground is named after yet another game loved by British cavalry officers in India?

358. Who did Floyd Patterson knock out in 1960 to regain the world heavyweight boxing championship?

359. Which footballer's real Christian names were Edson Orantes?

360. The US Open Golf tournament was first held at St Andrews Golf club in Yonkers in which year?

361. Sports journalist Henri Desgranges first organised which significant sporting event in 1903 as a publicity stunt for the magazine *L'Auto*?

362. In which year was a forward pass legalised in American football?

363. In which year did Rocky Marciano first take the world heavyweight title?

364. Which famous American boxer was born with the name Walker Smith?

365. In 1991 the British Football Association relaxed its rules to allow girls under what age to play in school team leagues?

366. Who did Billy Jean King beat in 1966 to take her first Wimbledon singles titles?

367. Alison Fisher and Stacey Hillyard are British champions, but in what?

368. In 1988 Reading AFC became the first league football team to acquire what?

369. In 1927 the council of Bishops in Germany successfully had banned a women's gymnastics festival, planned to take place in Neuberg an der Donau. But why?

370. Only one man has, to date (1994), won 109 tennis singles championships. Name him.

371. Joyce Wethered is the leading female exponent of which sport?

372. In 1728, Ann Field of Stoke Newington, London, challenged Elizabeth Stokes to what kind of contest?

373. In 1967, why was the Polish sprinter Eva Klobukowska stripped of all Olympic and other medals?

374. In April 1860, England's Tom Sayers and America's John Heenan met at Farnborough, Hampshire in the last of which type of sporting event to be staged in England?

375. Which was the first English team to win the European cup?

376. In which year were the Winter Olympics introduced?

377. Which tune is always played as the horses are trotted out for the Kentucky Derby?

378. To the nearest ounce, what is the weight of a lacrosse ball?

379. Lester Piggot romped home to win the 1970 Derby riding which horse?

380. Henry Cooper is famous for knocking Muhammed Ali onto the canvas but who actually broke his jaw?

381. In ice-skating, you see a double axel but how many turns does that include?

382. In 1974, Ander Haugen finally received the bronze medal he should have collected in 1924 – it took them that long to realise there had been a mistake in the scores. Which sport was it?

383. In 1971 a football stand collapsed killing sixty-six people. Name the ground.

384. Which Olympic track and field event do women not compete in?

385. Which Norwegian ski-ing champion was also an explorer, an oceanographer, a professor of zoology and an ambassador in the Diplomatic Corps?

386. The American World Series features which sport?

387. Which CB fanatic and Champion boxer uses the radio nickname of 'The Big Bopper'?

388. In which sport is the Lancôme Trophy awarded?

389. Who was the first woman to break the five minute mile?

390. Who set pace for Roger Bannister when he made his bid to break the four minute mile?

391. Name the only German to hold the world heavyweight championship?

392. Who became the first woman to win four successive US Open Tennis titles?

393. In the third week of July which event takes place on the River Thames?

394. For which sport is Carnoustie famous?

395. Which golf course was used for the first time in the 1977 British Open championships?

396. In how many hours of playing a top class chess match, do the players use as much energy as a football player in a ninety minute match?

397. The American Boston Bruins play which sport?

398. We all know Sir Donald Bradman repeatedly led the Australian cricket teams to victory but what country was he born in?

399. In sailing, what is a warp?

400. Who won the 1984 Stella Artois Tennis singles championships?

401. Name the horse owned by the Queen that won the 1977 St Leger?

402. Name by year the Olympics in which butterfly stroke races were first allowed. (This does not count its use in a freestlye race.)

403. What number did Roger Bannister have on his vest when he broke the four minute mile?

404. What was the old race track at Alexander Park nicknamed?

405. We all know Johnny Weissmuller played Tarzan,

but how many of the other Olympic swimmers who also took the role can you name? (One point each.)

406. There are two throwing events in the Heptathlon. What are they?

407. How many lanes are there in the standard Olympic swimming pool?

408. Gillian Sheen secured for England the first gold medal ever for which particular sport?

409. Every year Wentworth Golf Course plays host to which tournament?

410. Which British golf champion stood trial for attempted murder in 1970?

411. How did Brian Allen cross the Channel using pedal power?

412. Which wicket keeper has most often kept wicket for England?

413. Who took two swimming gold medals in the 1978 Commonwealth Games?

414. In 1950 Cambridge won the Boat Race, but who was their cox?

415. Which wicket keeper scored a century in the 1977 centenary test?

416. The teams of which sport compete for the Stanley Cup?

417. Which sporting equipment can be categorised as Gleneagles or Sandwich?

418. Jock Taylor was world champion in 1980 for which sport?

419. At the 1980 Winter Olympics Ingmar Stenmark took how many gold medals?

420. Which British sportsman is named after a Welsh geographical feature?

421. On the golf course we call it an albatross. What do the Americans call it?

422. Which test cricketer was the first president of the Bowling Association?

423. In golf, what is the term for a putt short enough to be conceded?

424. What do Newcastle United and Tottenham Hotspur have in common?

425. If the adjudicator in a judo match shouts 'Sonomama', what is required of the participants?

426. The Australian sporting fraternity call it a bosie. What do we call it?

427. Who was the first person in history to be recorded as owning a billiard table?

428. Who was the first person to receive the BBC's Sports Personality of the Year Award?

429. The motto of which sporting county is *Invicta*?

430. How much does a tennis ball weigh?

431. How old was Sonja Henie when she first won the World Figure Skating Championships?

432. In the 1960 Olympics, Wilma Rudolph took three gold medals at track events. Why was this considered something of an achievement?

433. How old was Emerson Fittipaldi when he first won the world Grand Prix Championship?

434. English jockeys Fred Archer and Lester Piggott have one achievement in common. What is it?

435. In 1980 John Hilton won the European championships of what sport?

436. What is the total number of Olympic gold medals accumulated by Russia between 1912 and 1952?

437. Which athlete became the first to take gold medals at the Olympic, European and Commonwealth games in the same series?

438. In the 1972 Olympics which favourite gymnast slipped on the parallel bars and received the shock score of 7.5?

439. Germany's best high jumper, Gretel Bergmann, was banned from the 1936 Olympics. Why?

440. In the north east of England lies the town of Killingworth. What is the name of that town's most famous daughter?

441. Which Olympic event for women was dropped in 1928 and not re-introduced until 1960?

442. In which year was cycling first allowed as a women's event in the Olympic Games?

443. American sprinter Helen Stephens won the 100 metres at the 1936 Olympics. What special little gift did Hitler give her?

444. Anita Porter – swimming gold medallist – became a correspondent for which newspaper?

445. The Greek calendar related everything to the Olympic register. In what year was this reckoned to have begun? (Allow a hundred years each way.)

446. In chess, what is the minimum number of moves in which white can achieve checkmate?

447. Victor Barna was five times world champion of which sport?

448. Who lit the flame for the 1956 Olympics and then broke eight world records?

449. At which of the modern Olympics did the Olympic flame make its appearance?

450. What is the longest greyhound race run in Britain?

451. How long is an Olympiad?

452. What is the maximum length of bandage a professional boxer can have on each hand?

453. Who took the part of Muhammed Ali in the bio-pic entitled *The Greatest*?

454. John McEnroe has only once won the men's doubles at Wimbledon. Who was his partner?

455. In 1979 Britain's Frankie Wainman took the World Championship at which sport?

456. Whom did Doreen Denny partner for ice-dancing?

457. Britain's Karen Corr is what type of champion?

458. In 1980 Tatyana Kazankina became the first woman to run what in less than four minutes?

459. Lynette Woodward and Jackie White made sporting history playing with which American team?

460. In which game do women compete for the Venice Bowl?

461. Over how many years did Sugar Ray Robinson's professional career stretch?

462. In the 1900 Olympic meetings at Paris, women were only allowed to compete in two events. Name them.

463. Who won the first boat race? (You have a fifty-fifty chance of being right, haven't you?)

464. The first world motor racing championships were staged where and in which year?

465. How old was Severiano Ballesteros when he first

entered the British Open and came second at Birkdale in 1976?

466. Which former England batsman died of a heart attack whilst touring with the English team in the West Indies in 1981?

467. Although Australian born, she held the British Open title for Squash for sixteen years solid between 1962 and 1977. What was her name?

468. In 1964 Tranmere Rovers scored a goal in four seconds from kickoff. Who were the Rovers playing?

469. Mrs Mary Outerbridge watched a game whilst vacationing in Bermuda and was so impressed that she introduced it to the USA. What was it?

470. Having been outlawed for drawing men away from the more useful skill of archery, in what year was cricket formally restored as being a legal pastime?

471. Name Denmark's most famous speedway star.

472. Willie Hammond plays cricket for which county?

473. In 1968 Leeds United became the first British club to win which cup?

474. In 1966 David Bryant took which world title?

475. Doubtless the most famous footballer this country

has ever produced, which position did Stanley Matthews play?

476. Pelotta is played in which country?

477. In a speed skating race at International level how many skaters are on the track at any one time?

478. Ronnie Peterson died at which motor racing track?

479. The Cesarewitch and the Cambridgeshire are together known as what?

480. Which jockey took Red Rum to victory in the 1977 Grand National?

481. In netball the rim of the net is set how high from the ground?

482. Although later famous as a heavyweight champion, in 1952 he was middleweight boxing gold medallist at the Olympics aged only seventeen. What was his name?

483. Athlete Tommy Smith became the first to do what in under twenty seconds?

484. In golf, what is the term to describe one who regularly plays below his real handicap?

485. On which British racecourse would you find the Rowley mile?

486. Who captained the American team for their first few ventures into the Ryder Cup?

487. Who did Stan Smith partner for Wimbledon men's doubles?

488. What is the national sport of Finland?

489. Which country was being toured by the British team in 1924 when they were first nicknamed 'The Lions'?

490. Which was the first English club to win the European cup?

491. In which sport might you perform a stem Christie?

492. Which horse took the Triple Crown in 1970?

493. Who was the founder member of America's swimming Hall of Fame?

494. What is the name of the baseball-like game involving a much larger ball which is pitched underarm?

495. In gymnastics, what kind of movement is a *tsukahara*?

496. Women's track and field events were introduced to the Olympics in which year?

497. In the 1949 British Open, Harry Bradshaw played a golf stroke now regarded as a classic. Where was the ball lying?

498. In which sport is the Lance Todd Memorial Trophy competed for?

499. Who captained England during the controversial 'Bodyline' tour?

500. Gordon Pirie took which British Championships in 1968?

501. In Ice Hockey what is the minimum period a player may be sent off to sit in the 'sin bin'?

502. Which flamboyant boxer became heavyweight champion of the world aged twenty-one?

503. Which country always leads the Olympic procession?

504. Which American baseball star was fornamed George Herman?

505. Which is the only Australian city to have hosted the Olympic games?

506. Jane Bridge became the first ever women's world champion at which sport?

507. What is Britain's longest cycling race?

508. What terminological contribution was made to British sporting jargon by a famous naval hero?

509. The sporting institution of BASI governs which body of professional sportspersons?

510. How many different ways can a batsman be 'out' at cricket?

511. How long is the rest period allowed between bouts in professional boxing?

512. The US Open tennis championships are held at Flushing Meadow but only since 1978. Prior to this where were they held?

513. In American rodeo competitions, how long must a rider stay on a bronco before he hears the bell?

514. The cricketer Bishan Bedi was famous for which speciality?

515. Which football team plays at Highbury?

516. What do the following players have in common: Orantes, Borg and Lendl?

517. Which country was represented at cricket by FW Woolley?

518. The Prince Phillip Cup is contested in which sport and in which location? (One point each.)

519. At which game does Gilliam Gilks excel?

520. Who, quite literally, brought much goodwill to the 1972 Olympics?

521. Which course was designed by former show-jumper Douglas Bunn?

522. What is Douglas Bunn's other great claim to fame?

523. Graham Noyce once excelled at which sporting activity?

524. How did Joan Bazely make footballing history?

525. Which sporting activity centres on the Palma Match?

526. Which infamous sporting event took place on February 8 1983?

527. Which brother and sister team took the mixed doubles trophy at Wimbledon in 1980?

528. When Torvill and Dean won their gold medal at the 1984 Olympics, what music were they skating to?

529. Which sportsman was knighted by the Queen whilst she was on a state visit to Barbados?

530. How many times was the 1979 Scottish FA Cup tie between Inverness Thistle and Falkirk postponed?

531. When the Grand National was run for the first time, what was it called?

532. Which yachtswoman sailed single-handed round the world in 1977/78?

533. Which woman was the youngest finalist in a professional tennis tournament?

534. In which 1981 sporting event did Dick Beardsley and Inge Simonsen cross the finishing line together?

535. Which piece of sports equipment is fitted as standard with sixteen feathers?

536. When did betting shops become legal in Britain?

537. Whose home ground is Old Deer Park?

538. How old was Ian Botham when he first played for Somerset?

539. Which boxer was known as 'The Boston Strong-boy'?

540. What happened to the Italian football team of Torino in 1949?

541. Which sportsman's nickname was Gentleman Jim?

542. Which country has most often won the Thomas Cup? (An extra point for the name of the sport.)

543. In golf, what is a Texas wedge?

544. Which piece of Olympic sporting equipment weighs exactly sixteen pounds?

545. By what name is Arnold Cream better known?

546. Name any one of the so-called Four Musketeers of French tennis in the twenties and thirties.

547. Judo was first competed at which Olympic games?

548. Why were women banned from watching the original Olympic Games? (If they were caught sneaking in disguised they were stoned to death.)

549. Which prominent sportsman was sued by his own fan club?

550. Who was the first American sportswoman to top $100,000 earnings in one year?

551. It was not to be his last FA Cup winner's medal but how old was Stanley Matthews when he won his first one?

552. Which sport is contested on a playing area 9 feet by 5 feet?

PEOPLE, PLACES AND EVENTS

1. Who was the first woman in history to be depicted on American currency?
2. The Spanish Armada. What does *Armada* mean?
3. Name any three of the Seven Wonders of the Ancient World.
4. Which king was married to Margaret of Anjou?
5. Who was the last monarch to be buried at Westminster Abbey?
6. Within three centuries either side, for how many centuries has the Japanese throne been occupied by a member of the same family?
7. Approximately how many years after his death did Edward, Prince of Wales, become known as 'The Black Prince'?

8. In which city would you find the Black Prince Interchange?

9. How many Tsars are buried in the Kremlin? (Accept any answer within five of the correct amount.)

10. Queen Berengaria never lived in or visited England. Which king was she married to?

11. Name either of the British monarchs who were crowned at the age of nine months.

12. In terms of area, which is the largest city in the US?

13. Approximately how many miles of shoreline does New York City have?

14. Which English philosopher drafted the constitution for South Carolina?

15. Who wrote. 'I do not trust any Russian. As soon as a Russian worms his way in, all hell breaks loose'?

16. Which Cape is at the southernmost tip of Africa?

17. Before the great Reform Act, how many members of Parliament did Old Sarum have?

18. What was the real name of Ulysses Simpson Grant?

19. When was Bolivia liberated from Spanish rule? (Allow any answer within ten years of the correct date.)

20. In which century was 25 December first celebrated as the birth date of Christ?

21. In which decade did it become acceptable to affirm, rather than take, an oath on the Bible in the English Courts?

22. Where are the Calendar Islands?

23. Which three states in the USA have active volcanoes?

24. Whose assassin went by the alias Jacques van den Dreschd?

25. Which 18th century prime minister was described by Lady Mary Montagu as 'The Potent Knight whose Belly goes At Least a Yard before his Nose'?

26. In which country is Lake Titicaca?

27. In which British county would you find Great Torrington?

28. Tosks and Ghegs are the major ethnic and linguistic divisions of which European country?

29. Who commanded the French and Spanish fleet at the Battle of Trafalgar?

30. Which mountain range is also known as the Southern Carpathians?

31. In which county does the River Trent rise and which estuary does it empty into?

32. Ghana has an artificial lake begun in 1961 and finished in 1965. What is its name?

33. In which century was the title 'Prince of Wales' created?

34. Which county was Wallingford in before the 1974 reorganisation?

35. What name is given to the area of New York that extends for seven blocks from Broadway to the East River?

36. Name any three counties that border Warwickshire.

37. Where in England was the first crematorium set up?

38. The flag of which country comprises three horizontal stripes – red, white, black – and a blue triangle with a red star in it?

39. On which river would you find the Zongo rapids?

40. In January 1993, what controversial cargo was carried by the freighter Akatsuki Maru?

41. What institution celebrated its millenium in Russia during June 1988?

42. Who shouted out to Pope John Paul II, 'I renounce you as the Antichrist'?

43. When Aileen Wuornos went on trial in America what was she accused of?

44. For which exploit did Matthias Rust become famous?

45. Whose daughter is Alina Fernandez Revuelta?

46. Who was George Bush's opponent in the 1988 presidential race?

47. Which natural disaster struck the Sudan in 1988?

48. Files relating to which major incident were made public in the US in August 1993?

49. How did Pakistan's military ruler President Zia Ul'Haq die?

50. Electorally, what was different about 1918, 1922, 1924 and 1931?

51. What part of London is designated SW19?

52. What nationality was Dr Crippen?

53. What type of car was James Dean driving when he met his death?

54. According to *Forbes* magazine, who was the world's highest paid sportsman in 1993?

55. Who were Catherine Eddowes, Mary Ann Kelly and Annie Chapman?

56. What do the following have in common: the Age of Steam; British postcards; D-Day and the Channel Tunnel?

57. How many people were killed in the Valentine's Day Massacre?

58. Who won £5,000 from *The Times* which printed a letter implicating him in the Phoenix Park murders?

59. According to the United Nations' Children's Fund, which country has the highest rate of teenage suicide in the industrialised world?

60. What was draped over the obelisk in Paris' Place de la Concorde on December 1 1993?

61. Who was the first British astronaut?

62. Approximately how much money was raised for charity by the 118 men and women who walked through the newly completed Channel Tunnel?

63. When astronaut Sergei Krikolev arrived back on earth, what didn't exist anymore?

64. What lake is the source of the Mississippi?

65. Which rank in the navy is also known as a Flag Officer?

66. What is U3A short for?

67. What is the name for the stretch of water between the coast of Africa and Madagascar?

68. Fashion and cosmetics house Yves St Laurent were told to change the name of one of their perfumes in December 1993. Why?

69. Approximately how many thousand years ago did the Sahara begin to dry up?

70. The motto of which American state is 'North To The Future'?

71. What is the capital of New York state?

72. How old was Prince Albert when he died?

73. In which organisation are members identified by first name and a last initial?

74. Where is the Aldan River?

75. In what decade was the Aldershot military training centre established?

76. Which islands stretch in a 1,700 mile arc and finish up with 500 miles of the Kamchatka Peninsula?

77. Which monarch ordered Cabot to explore America?

78. Which country is drained by the Valira River and its tributaries?

79. Who was the first monarch of Great Britain and Ireland?

80. How did Anne Bonney achieve fame or more accurately, notoriety?

81. Approximately how many so-called 'Anti-Popes' have there been?

82. In the US what is the purpose of Arbor Day?

83. What is the smallest county in Northern Ireland?

84. On which Scottish island would you find the villages of Brodick and Lamlash?

85. What group of people communicate in the Athapaskan languages?

86. Which ruler is represented in the head of the Great Sphinx?

87. Which American poet's grandfather founded Washington University?

88. Which order of monks used Tintern Abbey?

89. Approximately how many feet below sea level is the Caspian Sea?

90. Which mountain used to be known merely as Peak XV?

91. When was the British Exchequer abolished?

92. Everyone knows about the *Enola Gay* but what was the name of the B-29 that dropped the second atomic bomb on Nagasaki?

93. Still with the bomb, Nagasaki was actually the secondary target, the intended target was obscured owing to bad weather. What was the name of the town?

94. How many spikes are there on the Statue of Liberty's crown?

95. Which reference work is dedicated to Bill Clinton and Queen Elizabeth II?

96. Approximately how many Oxford colleges have the same name as Cambridge colleges?

97. Which Pacific island, 1,350 miles southeast of Tahiti, was named for the sailor who first sighted it?

98. Which six towns are given the collective name of 'The Potteries'?

99. Which two counties were amalgamated in 1974 to form Powys?

100. In which county is Romney Marsh?

101. The name of which New Zealand city is taken from the Maori for 'two lakes', 'second lake' or 'lake of the pit'?

102. Which vessel finished its last commercial voyage at the Falkland Islands in May, 1886?

103. Who was probably the last person to be offered a dukedom but turned it down for fear it would damage the political prospects of his son and grandson?

104. The London to Brighton car rally was established in November 1896. What was being celebrated by its inauguration?

105. What tax was finally abolished on July 24 1851?

106. Which Royal Palace has the distinction of being the last one to be sold?

107. For how long did the Bow Street Runners exist?

108. On the royal coat of arms, England is represented by three golden lions on a red background. What colour are their claws and tongues?

109. When William IV died, which crown did Victoria *not* inherit?

110. Who was the last British monarch to use their power to dismiss a government?

111. Frances Stuart, Duchess of Richmond and mistress of Charles II, was the inspiration for an image that is in use even today. What is the image?

112. Which parliament sat for the last time on August 2 1800?

113. Which British spa town was known to the Romans as Aquae Armentiae?

114. What name is given to the deepest point in the Atlantic ocean?

115. In which year did Milton Keynes come into being?

116. For approximately how many centuries did the period now known as the Middle Ages last?

117. What is the name given to August 24 1662 – the day on which Charles II barred 2,000 Non-conformist ministers from their posts?

118. Two American states have cities called El Dorado. Name one of them?

119. The Eighty Years War was fought to secure one country's independence from another. Can you name either of the countries?

120. Which island in the eastern Pacific is also known as Rapanui?

121. What was the cause of the 19th century Cotton Famine?

122. Where is the Coromandel Peninsula?

123. Name any three states in the area of the US known as the Corn Belt.

124. What is the collective name given to the Rockies, the Sierra Nevada and the mountains in between them?

125. In which year of the Second World War did the Battle of the Coral Sea take place?

126. On the banks of which river does the Cheshire town of Congleton stand?

127. What was the first name of Christopher Columbus's eldest son?

128. The troops of which nation first opened fire on the French mob to kick off the big revolution?

129. George Washington lost all his teeth early and had a false set made from teeth taken from what dead animal?

130. Prince William of Gloucester became the first member of the Royal Family to get what on the January 5 1965?

131. John O'Groats and Land's End are not the most northern and southern points in Great Britain. A point each for the true claimants for the titles.

132. Many politicians and statesmen have talked of an Iron Curtain, long before Churchill. They were all drawing on a particular metaphor based on what?

133. What was the original name of The White House?

134. Which sweet-toothed French king appointed a Royal Chocolatier to whizz out his bedtime drinks?

135. Which national heroine of Victorian England did, in reality, spend the last fifty years of her life in bed, a hopeless drug addict and hypochondriac?

136. What did Florence Nightingale always carry in the pocket of her nursing dress?

137. Florence Nightingale did not carry the type of lamp traditionally associated with her. The one she really did carry was standard issue to which nation's army?

138. In America in 1936, everybody knew the name Bruno Hauptmann. Why?

139. The name of the Cenotaph takes its name from Greek but what does it mean?

140. What was the name of Napoleon's charger?

141. What do the following have in common: Stacey Keach, Sophia Loren, Robert Mitchum and Steve McQueen?

142. Which of the Marx brothers was a deaf mute?

143. What do the following have in common: Elvis Presley, George II and Catherine the Great of Russia?

144. In the Victorian era, the most popular colour for a wedding dress was what?

145. Name the 79th person to fly the Atlantic.

146. What do the following have in common: Anne Boleyn, Lady Jane Grey, Catherine Howard, Lady Rochford, Countess of Salisbury and the Earl of Essex?

147. The state of Pennsylvania is believed to be named after William Penn the Quaker. It is not. For whom was it named?

148. On his second journey across the Atlantic which island did Columbus find?

149. What was the name of the submarine that torpedoed the *General Belgrano*?

150. Who were Patrick Pearse, Joseph Plunkett and James Connolly?

151. Which British politician declined a visit from Queen Victoria on his deathbed saying: 'No, she will only ask me to take a message to Albert'?

152. What was the name of the liner which came to the aid of passengers from the stricken *Titanic*?

153. Which General ordered the invasion of the Falkland Islands?

154. Which highly controversial object was unloaded

from a Bahamas-registered merchantman called the *Gur Mariner*?

155. Which president signed the resolution which took the US into the First World War?

156. Which British historian said: 'Power tends to corrupt, and absolute power corrupts absolutely'?

157. Which outlaw was allegedly shot in the back of the head whilst he was hanging a picture?

158. What was the name of the super-tanker which ran aground in Prince William Sound, Alaska?

159. Which prime minister broke down on television whilst he was confessing to adultery?

160. How was Tsar Alexander II murdered?

161. What ceased to be legal at midnight on March 11 1983?

162. Which of Hitler's right-hand men said: 'The Americans cannot build aeroplanes. They are very good at refrigerators and razor blades'?

163. How many years' imprisonment was Gavrilo Princip sentenced to for his assassination of Archduke Ferdinand?

164. In 1973 which British pop star was charged with growing marijuana on his Scottish farm?

165. In which year was the Locarno Pact signed?

166. The famous Red Indian princess Pocahontas is buried where?

167. Which country's name means The Land of the People with the Big Feet?

168. What did Admiral Horatio Nelson and American gangster George 'Baby Face' Nelson have in common?

169. In which year did the last military engagement between America and Great Britain occur?

170. How many Popes have been murdered?

171. Who qualifies as the youngest president of the United States?

172. How were witches executed in 'merrie' England?

173. Which public office takes its name from a prominent figure in a fox hunt?

174. Where did Guy Fawkes place his gunpowder?

175. Which city took its nickname from the Spanish word *manzana*?

176. Female pirates Anne Bonney and Mary Read escaped the gallows. How?

177. Which urban area has the greatest population?

178. What is the name of Hong Kong's stock exchange?

179. Who was the leader of the Branch Davidian sect?

180. Who was sworn in as the Prime Minister of Canada in June 1993 only to lose the position a mere four months later?

181. In November 1993, Vice President Al Gore dedicated a war memorial to a branch of the armed services who served during the Vietnam War. Which branch was it?

182. What finally took effect on November 1 1993?

183. The 1994 floods in America's Mid-west caused an estimated $12 billion worth of damage. Approximately how great a percentage of these were covered by insurance?

184. In 1991, who said: 'The great, the jewel and the mother of battles has begun'?

185. Apart from being fighting dogs, what do the dogo Argentino and the fila Braziliera have in common?

186. Who was the author of the controversial book *Spycatcher*?

187. According to his former Chief of Staff, how did Ronald Reagan choose the dates for his meetings with world leaders?

188. Which organisation was founded in 1961 by British lawyer Peter Benenson?

189. The ABC powers is a term applied collectively to which three nations?

190. In 1994 which European country asked Prince Edward to assume their throne?

191. Who said: 'Arms alone are not enough to keep the peace – it must be kept by men'?

192. Who was installed as President of the Philippines in February, 1986?

193. A suffragette went on trial accused of bombing Lloyd George's villa. Who was she?

194. In which year did Adolf Hitler become a German citizen?

195. Which British monarch was excommunicated by Pope Pius V?

196. Which city lies 25 miles north-west of the Hoover Dam?

197. The husband of Lady Caroline Lamb went on to be Queen Victoria's first Prime Minister. Who was he?

198. In terms of surface area which is the largest lake in the world?

199. In Britain there are knights, in France, chevaliers. What is the equivalent in Germany?

200. Three boroughs and one town were formed into the borough Kingston-upon-Thames in 1965. Name any two of them.

201. Who was the first Queen's Counsel?

202. What is the state capital of Kentucky?

203. During which year of the Second World War did the first kamikaze mission take place?

204. In Canada which date is Dominion Day?

205. Which of the Twelve Apostles is venerated as the patron of lost causes or impossible things?

206. Who married Princess Sofia of Greece in 1962?

207. In 1981, what was retrieved from the hull of the British cruiser *Edinburgh*?

208. Whereabouts was Che Guevara when he was shot dead?

209. In September 1976, how much did the British Treasury borrow from the International Monetary Fund?

210. In the contest for the Tory leadership, who were the candidates in the second and, as it turned out, final ballot?

211. In which month and year did Margaret Thatcher resign as leader of the Conservative party?

212. Who quit his post as Secretary of State for Trade and Industry after his anti-German remarks were reported in the *Spectator* magazine?

213. Which of the Great Train Robbers was shot dead at the side of his swimming pool in Marbella?

214. Which leader built a commune in Oregon and owned ninety-three Rolls Royces?

215. In January 1990, who was elected the first woman general secretary of the Communist Party of Great Britain?

216. Which MP was found guilty of criminal damage after he had wrecked the flat of his ex-mistress?

217. In July 1991, the wives of leaders attending the G7 economic summit made a series of visits to various venues. Which of them accompanied the Princess of Wales to visit patients with HIV?

218. Which was the first Royal Navy ship to carry female personnel at sea?

219. Who was appointed as France's first woman prime minister?

220. According to the judge who tried the case, who showed herself to be 'a calm, composed, deliberate and unblushing liar'?

221. Who served five years of a ten year sentence in an Iranian prison and said on his release: 'Anyone who has been educated in an English public school and survived in the ranks of the British Army feels at home in a Third World prison'?

222. What was the last battle for which the British high command seriously considered the use of massed archers?

223. Which woman completed a 10,000 mile trek across Africa on September 1 1993?

224. Which country stages an annual tomato fight?

225. HMS *Tamar* is set in the heart of which city's financial district?

226. Which country's army banned discrimination against gay men and women in June 1993?

227. In 1993, who was reported to have insured his taste buds for £250,000?

228. Who sued whom over a 'dirty tricks campaign'?

229. Captain Oates ended his life during Scott's Polar Expedition. What was his Christian name?

230. Who finished off his journal with the words: 'It seems a pity, but I do not think I can write more – for God's sake look after our people'?

231. Which two ships were the first to leave Portsmouth to join the Falklands Task Force?

232. Who married Baronness Marie von Reibnitz?

233. What were the names of the two women founders of the Ulster Peace Movement?

234. Which prime minister resigned with no prior warning and instructed his press secretary to: 'Tell the lobby correspondents you've got a little story that might interest them'?

235. The Chinese emperor Ch'in Shih-huang-ti created three lasting and world famous things for his country; one was the name China. Name one of the others.

236. How is Richard John Bingham better and more infamously known?

237. Juan Peron's second wife became President of Argentina after his death. What was her name?

238. Which British chemical plant blew up spectacularly in June 1974?

239. In the 1974 Local Government reorganisation, how many of the forty-five English counties remained unchanged?

240. What was the name of the group that kidnapped Patty Hearst?

241. What regiment's uniform did Captain Mark Phillips wear for his marriage to Princess Anne?

242. At which event did Princess Anne and Mark Phillips announce their engagement?

243. What was Winston Churchill's second name?

244. On what day of the week is Thanksgiving always celebrated?

245. In 1972 who was the Democratic challenger for the US presidency?

246. When was shaving of the head abolished for monks in Catholic Orders?

247. Which Home Secretary resigned over his involvement with architect John Poulson?

248. Of which infamous leader did a British Home Office official say: 'We always thought that he was a decent chap. After all he served in the British Army for more than fifteen years'?

249. What was thrown at Edward Heath by an irate protester as he went to sign the Treaty of Brussels?

250. On Armistice Day, World War One, what was the last town taken by American troops?

251. How many islands are there in the Faroe Islands group?

252. How many oceans are there?

253. Only two capital cities lie north of the 60 degree parallel. What are they? (One point each.)

254. Name the world's first completely evacuated city?

255. French President Giscard d'Estaing invited an entire Alsatian village to dine with him at the Elysée Palace. Why?

256. Timbuktu lies in which country?

257. How many South American countries have no coastline? (One point each for their names?)

258. If you found yourself in Goodnews Bay, what country would you be in?

259. The Philippines is an archipelago of many islands. Approximately how many?

260. Who owned the jail that came to be known as the Black Hole of Calcutta?

261. Which is the world's largest island?

262. We've all heard of Martha's Vineyard but what is it and where is it?

263. What separates New York from Vermont?

264. Which river runs through Berlin?

265. In 1906 the Rodeo Land and Water Company laid out what?

266. Which country produces the largest potato crop?

267. What is the circumference of the earth at the equator?

268. What kind of vessel will the New Zealand authorities not allow to dock in any of its ports?

269. China may be the biggest but what is the second biggest country in the world?

270. The town of Climax, Colorado is famous for what?

271. The furthest city from the sea is to be found

where? (One point for the city and another for the number of miles from nearest coastline?)

272. Which European city has the greatest mileage of canals?

273. Israel and Jordan share which body of water?

274. On average, how many earthquakes rack Japan in the course of a year?

275. Where is the home of the bird of paradise?

276. Six hundred million acres of the world's arable land is given over to the production of what?

277. What percentage of Spain is arid and useless (excluding Benidorm!)?

278. Geographically, which state lies at the centre of the United States?

279. What do Pakistan and Israel have in common?

280. How many independent nations make up South America?

281. Which of the world's capitals is the highest above sea level?

282. Between them Alaska, Chile and Iceland encompass half the world's what?

283. The ancient kingdom of Mesopotamia is now contained within which modern state?

284. How many official languages are spoken in

Switzerland and what are they? (One point for three, two points for all four.)

285. Which Australian city grew out of a convict settlement called Edenglassie?

286. What is the largest fruit crop of America?

287. In 1984, Upper Volta was renamed. What is it called now?

288. Prior to the American Civil War what was the capital city of the Confederate south?

289. Before the Falklands Conflict, Britain had to demand an Argentinian withdrawal from which other island group and when?

290. When the Russians sold Alaska to America for $7 million it was a con. Why?

291. Name the body of water which separates North America from Asia.

292. Which major country has the longest uninterrupted Royal line?

293. Which country was so named by Spanish explorers who saw houses built on stilts over rivers and tributaries?

294. Named after Hitler, the drug Adolphine is today better known by what name?

295. The name of which Caribbean island was coined because of all the bearded fig trees found there?

296. Between the tip of South Africa and the Antarctic coast is found Bouvet Island. Who owns it?

297. Vientiana is the capital of which country?

298. Which country has the most active volcanoes in the world?

299. What is the new name of Rangoon?

300. The legislative body of which island is called The States of Deliberation?

301. Which is larger, Monaco or New York's Central Park?

302. There are two South American countries in OPEC. Name them. (One point for each.)

303. Name the only two European cities built on seven hills.

304. What separates Oman from Iran?

305. What is moving closer to the North Pole at a rate of 9.3 metres per annum?

306. Which South American country is the main tin producer?

307. Which country has no legislative system of its own, and is governed purely by international law?

308. Where is Mount Erebus?

309. Although now united, in which year was Germany formally divided into two Republics?

310. There is only one Portuguese speaking country in South America. Which one is it?

311. In which country is the oldest commercial newspaper published?

312. Which river contains more water than the rivers Nile, Yangtze and Mississippi combined?

313. The Rainbow Bridge spans which river?

314. What is the only country in the world to contain the Equator and a Tropic?

315. Which country is the smallest independent state in the world?

316. The Russian city of Stalingrad changed its name to what?

317. In which American state would you find the Black Canyon?

318. What is the highest capital city of Europe?

319. At its widest, how wide is Chile?

320. The state of Denmark comprises many off-shore islands. Approximately how many?

321. Which was the first city built to plan and not just allowed to grow as it pleased?

322. Name the world's biggest importer of wheat.

323. Adolf Hitler had a hideaway called the Eagle's Nest in the mountains above which German city?

324. What is the name of the oldest continually inhabited French town?

325. What was named after Sir Benjamin Hall?

326. Name the largest of the Solomon Islands.

327. How many South American countries do not share a border with Brazil?

328. Which country is the world's largest producer of corn (the crop variety)?

329. In which American city would you find the famous Sugar Bowl?

330. What percentage of Greece is given over to arable farming?

331. Who met at Castle Chinon in 1429?

332. Which city did Beethoven make his home?

333. Which country is the world's largest exporter of electricity?

334. Which country doles out the most overseas aid?

335. Where would you find the Grasshopper Glacier?

336. The Necropolis of Vissovi is found in which disputed state?

337. Which Canadian province is the major producer of maple syrup?

338. What is the capital of Nepal?

339. Which nation was refused admission to the United Nations until 1955 because of its Nazi sympathies during World War Two?

340. New Zealanders are outnumbered by their sheep but by how many to one?

341. Which American city is dominated by a massive statue of the Roman god Vulcan, which peers down menacingly from Red Mountain?

342. By what name is the Orellana River better known today?

343. How many official languages are there in Peru?

344. Which area of the US was invaded and held by the Japanese during the Second World War?

345. Which Russian premier had a degree in metallurgic engineering?

346. Which country is called 'the breadbasket of the world'?

347. What city in the US has the highest car per person ratio?

348. What is the largest country in the Southern Hemisphere?

349. Approximately how many steps per minute are taken by a British soldier executing quick march?

350. To the nearest thousand, how many slaves were

released upon the issue of Lincoln's Emancipation Bill?

351. In 1915, Mr Chubb, a Wiltshire farmer, bought Mrs Chubb a unique present for £6,600. What was it?

352. When did France abolish the Guillotine?

353. How was Reza Pahlavi better known?

354. Who was the first American saint?

355. When Jackie Bouvier married John Kennedy, what was her occupation?

356. Queen Wilhelmina of the Netherlands abdicated in September 1948 – in favour of whom?

357. Where was Mother Teresa born?

358. The Suffragette Movement in the USA began campaigning in 1869. How long did it take before the US legislature gave women the right to vote?

359. On which beach did the following notice appear in 1979: 'Clothes Need Not Be Worn Beyond This Notice'?

360. Trinidadian Prime Minister A R Robinson and other hostages were held by Muslim rebels during July 1990. In which high profile building were they detained?

361. What are Prince William's other Christian names?

362. In what year were women ordained priests of the Anglican Church?

363. A major event caused Prime Minister Margaret Thatcher to say: 'Britain is great again'. What was the occasion?

364. In June 1986 two non-British citizens were given honorary knighthoods. One was Bob Geldof, who was the other?

365. Name all five of the D-Day landing beaches.

366. What were the Christian names of Casanova?

367. Lord Kitchener died when the ship carrying him on a mission to Russia hit a mine and sank. What was the name of the ship?

368. After his abdication, how long did the Duke of Windsor wait to marry Wallis Simpson?

369. What was introduced on May 1935?

370. Who was living in Argentina under the assumed name Ricardo Klement?

371. Who was the first Western pop star to play in the USSR?

372. How many of Henry VIII's wives were still living after his death?

373. Why did the biblical book of Leviticus take on such importance for Henry VIII?

374. Norman Shelley made some famous speeches

during the 1940s which caused something of a stir in the media world fifty years later. Why?

375. What was the first name of Mick Jagger's first wife?

376. Who was Claretta Petacci?

377. How was Mussolini killed?

378. Which Californian town elected Clint Eastwood as its Mayor?

379. Marlon Brando refused his 1973 Oscar as a protest against what?

380. In what year was the last Cruise missile at Greenham Common airbase moved to be dismantled?

381. In which decade did the Boers declare the Transvaal a republic?

382. In which year did F W de Klerk revoke Nelson Mandela's life sentence?

383. Which was the first country to leave the EEC?

384. In which year did the last full scale cavalry charge take place? (An extra point for where.)

385. Which branch of the services is named from the Latin meaning 'unable to speak'?

386. Which military insignia of rank survives as a symbol of experience of warfare at the joust?

387. Which service-rank indicates that the holder used to lead a band of robbers and cut-throats?

388. Which famous torturer had a surname which in part described what he did for a living?

389. Which Roman emperor was named for his footwear?

390. A famous hotel in Nashville, Tennessee gave its name to its own blend of a certain product. It is still bought today. What is it?

391. After the Battle of Culloden in 1746, what was outlawed under pain of death?

392. The town of Conestoga in Pennsylvania produced the covered wagons which opened up the American West. What was their nickname?

393. When the Roman Catholic church considers a candidate for sainthood, they appoint a Cardinal to oppose the motion, almost as in a court of law; the opposing cardinal is known by what title?

394. Name a geographical feature which is a third of a million square miles larger than the main body of the USA, excluding Alaska.

395. In the Holy Lands there is a plant known as the fraxinella – it lies at the centre of a famous biblical yarn. By what name is it better known?

396. There is a town in Great Britain which used to be

specifically included or excluded in declarations of war against this country. What is it?

397. In what year did the Great Fire of Chicago strike?

398. We've all heard of the Wars of the Roses between the houses of York and Lancaster. Which was red and which was white?

399. Which Pope died after absentmindedly drinking poisoned wine he had prepared to rid himself of an irksome cardinal?

400. How many years ago (allow ten or fifteen either way) was the so-called Star of David officially adopted by the Judaic peoples?

401. What do Prime Minister John Major's parents have in common with actor Burt Lancaster?

402. Garibaldi – saviour and unifier of Italy – was born in which country?

403. Presidents Kennedy and Lincoln were both assassinated on the same day of the week. Which was it?

404. Good King Zog was the last monarch of which country?

405. Where was the Empress Josephine born?

406. Between the years of 1788 and 1820 all productions of King Lear were banned in Britain. Why?

407. 'What is the use of a WC without a seat?': of whom was this said and why?

408. Queen Victoria was the longest reigning British monarch, but for how many years was it?

409. In 1695 a new fashion for men hit the streets of London. What was it?

410. Who was introduced to whom on January 10 1931 at Burrough Court, Leicestershire?

411. In September 1552, Henry III received an unusual present from Norway which he used to exercise in the River Thames. What was it?

412. In 1797 James Hetherington was arrested in London for disturbing the peace, having taken to the London streets sporting a new fashion of his own design. What was it?

413. In 1580 which new song was top of the pops?

414. Who was executed at Fotheringay on February 8 1587?

415. Which public facility was first opened at Bishopsgate, London in 1635?

416. Which government 'U-turn' was announced on April 23 1991?

417. Which major demolition project began on the night of November 9 1989?

418. In which year did the IRA bomb the London Stock Exchange?

419. Which political initiative of global importance was instituted in February 1986?

420. In May 1725, London's master criminal and public enemy number one was executed at Tyburn. What was his name?

421. Within the nearest ten years when did the War of Austrian Succession begin?

422. Exactly three minutes after Ronald Reagan had finished his inauguration speech, which group of prisoners were released and by whom?

423. On August 2 1784, the first mail coach service was established in this country. Between which two cities did it run?

424. Which event was captured in a book published by Salman Rushdie in 1981?

425. In 1707 a retired footman of Queen Anne found himself a business partner and opened what in London's Piccadilly?

426. On May 2 1895, Oscar Wilde was imprisoned in Reading Gaol. What was his sentence?

427. On July 2 1865, William Booth held a meeting in London's Whitechapel district. This was the beginning of which organisation?

428. Who arrived in Scutari on November 4 1854?

429. In 1846, which British city became the first outside London to open public parks?

430. Which two commanders were given a serious spanking at the Battle of Actium?

431. Anne Sullivan was a teacher with an internationally famous pupil. What was the pupil's name?

432. Napoleon's horse was called Marengo, Alexander the Great's Bucephalus, but whose nag was called Brigham?

433. In 1870 Napoleon III organised a national competition to find a substitute for which product?

434. Genesis, Exodus, Leviticus, Numbers and Deuteronomy are the first five books of the Bible collectively known by which name?

435. How many pilgrims sailed on the Mayflower in 1620?

436. What is the official language of Liechtenstein?

437. Which British king died after his horse tripped over a mole hill?

438. Which historical character has been portrayed in morc films than any other?

439. What is Dennis Healey's middle name?

440. There are several mountains called Olympus on earth, but there is another one. Where?

441. Which British monarch reigned for ten years but only spent five months in the country?

442. The speaker of the House of Commons may be

a powerful position but only one has ever been made a saint. Name him.

443. Which Tsar met Charles II?

444. Alfred Packer became the first man in America to be convicted of which crime?

445. What was the name of Punch's dog?

446. The American state of Georgia was founded in 1733 as a depository for which particular type of prisoner?

447. A certain gentleman by the name of Bumper Harris was employed by the early London underground to do what?

448. The Motor Car act of 1903 fixed an upper speed limit on all open roads throughout the country. What was that limit?

449. By which collective name are the trio of Melchior, Balthazzar and Caspar better known?

450. What was Harold Macmillan's first name?

451. Who was George III's granddaughter?

452. Who was L B Johnson's vice-president from 1964 to 1966?

453. Which British monarch was an internationally recognised philatelist?

454. Name the inventor of the exploding shell who

also contributed to other developments in artillery.

455. Apart from Oxford and Cambridge, name two other British universities that operate on a collegiate system.

456. What claim to fame does the village of Meriden have?

457. Which Victorian chancellor introduced the Inheritance Tax?

458. In which year was the BBC Third Programme (now Radio 3) launched to give listeners more variety?

459. The state of Liberia was founded as a haven for emancipated slaves wishing to return to Africa from the United States, but what was that nation found to be trafficking in 1930?

460. The S S *Titanic* sank in 1912. Which company owned the vessel?

461. What do the group called the Guardian Angels do?

462. When did tea rationing end in Britain?

463. In 1951 central Coventry became Britain's first what?

464. In 1952 Queen Elizabeth proclaimed that her children and grandchildren would bear what?

465. In which year was Louise Brown born?

466. In which year was Ceausescu executed in Romania?

467. Which year saw the first major finds of natural gas in the North Sea?

468. Who was knighted at Greenwich on July 7 1967?

469. Who was fatally wounded in Los Angeles in 1968?

470. Who was shot dead in St James's Square in 1984?

471. Who was killed whilst on holiday in County Sligo in 1979?

472. What did Arthur Wellesley win in 1815?

473. In which year did women over thirty get the vote in Britain?

474. Who was sentenced to ninety-nine years in 1969 for the murder of Martin Luther King?

475. What was confirmed at a ceremony in Lille, on January 20 1986?

476. For which abortive invasion did President Kennedy accept personal responsibility in 1961?

477. The Swedish prime minister was assassinated in 1986. What was his name?

478. Supersonic flight was first achieved in what year?

479. How did the Statue of Liberty celebrate her 100th birthday?

480. In what year did Ceylon become Sri Lanka?

481. Who met on the British warship *Fearless* in 1968?

482. Who crowned himself in 1967 and proclaimed his wife, Farah, to be divine empress?

483. What was the name given to October 19 1987?

484. Why was President Clinton forced to drop his nomination of Zoe Baird for attorney general?

485. The Battle of Lepanto of 1571 was the last conflict of which kind?

486. In 19th century China what served as currency?

487. History has seen many would-be world dominators, amongst them Alexander the Great, Napoleon, Hitler – but which conqueror took control of the largest area of land?

488. Who instituted and opened the first public library in London?

489. Why are there no Crown Jewels or regalia predating Charles II?

490. Very much in the ancient world a famous battle

took place at a location whose name meant 'hot gates'. Where was it? (Think about it, it's not that difficult.)

491. During the mid-18th century which product formed the bulk of contraband bought into this country?

492. In 218 BC, Hannibal crossed two mountain ranges. Name them both.

493. What did the following monarchs have in common: William II, Charles I and George VI?

494. Which two men staged a wrestling match at the field of the Cloth of Gold in 1520?

495. How many acquittals were there at the Nuremberg War Crimes trials?

496. In which year in Britain was the legal marriageable age of a girl raised from twelve?

497. What began at eight p.m. every night during the reign of William the Conquerer?

498. For how long was Mary, Queen of Scots, held prisoner in England before her execution?

499. Which famous writer helped to organise the Spanish Armada?

500. Henry VII decreed that all law courts of the land should start to use what?

501. The people of which country instituted the cheese manufacturing business in Britain?

502. Who did Ramon Mercadr kill on August 20 1940?

503. Why did Heroo Onoda hide out on the Philippines island of Lubang for nearly thirty years?

504. What type of pet did Lord Byron keep in his rooms at Cambridge University?

505. In reality, King John did not sign the Magna Carta. Why not?

506. In all, how many children did Queen Victoria have?

507. Who startled Americans by chopping up saloons with a hatchet?

508. Which early 14th century Frenchman moved north to rally and unify the Scots?

509. In 1907 Florence Nightingale became the first woman to receive what?

510. Yo-yos were banned in Damascus in 1933. Why?

511. What did Captain Lindemann lose in 1941?

512. The second and sixth presidents of America had the same surname. What was it?

513. Who was the first American president to resign?

514. Up until 1982, what metal, specifically, was used to make Victoria Crosses?

515. Which British monarch was the first to carry the title Prince of Wales?

516. When Marco Polo wrote his famous memoirs, where was he?

517. In Roman times what separated the Forth and the Clyde?

518. The War of the Roses opened with a fierce battle at which location?

519. Which American president invented the first folding bed?

520. Who introduced ginger, pepper and sugar to this country?

521. In what decade did the British Army retire the last of its mules?

522. Who was in charge of the English fleet sent up against the Armada?

523. Which Queen was dressed and reared as a boy, ruled for twenty-two years and finally abdicated?

524. What did the Doge of early Venice throw into the sea in a yearly ceremony?

525. What was Mrs Wallis Simpson's middle name?

526. Who was the last viceroy of India?

527. How were the bodies of dead Crusaders preserved for their homeward journey?

528. What did Nelson lose at Santa Cruz?

529. Why were the pilgrims in Chaucer's tales heading to Canterbury?

530. Who was nicknamed Corporal Violet?

531. What began on June 25 1950?

532. The crew of the spaceship *Endeavour* established a NASA record for space walks, but what were they actually doing up there?

533. What was the religion of England during the Middle Ages?

534. Who was thrown out of West Point in 1831 for turning out to inspection drunk and naked?

535. Who was the first King of Great Britain?

536. Who rode Black Nell?

537. In November 1993, which public school appointed a foreigner as a headmaster for the first time since its founding?

538. The site of Rudolph Hess's grave was revealed in 1993. Where is it?

539. In 1993 which company announced that it had lost $900 million dollars in its first year of business?

540. Which public attraction admitted Screaming Lord Sutch as one of its first visitors on August 7 1993?

541. In July 1993, what were Cubans allowed to possess that had been denied to them for many years previously?

542. Who is the female boss of MI5?

543. A statue of whom was unveiled by the Queen Mother in London on June 23 1993?

544. In 1994 which British oil refinery exploded injuring twenty-six plant workers?

545. Launched in America in 1993, what is the 'Toys for Guns' scheme?

546. Who was the first UN leader to cross the border from South to North Korea?

547. In 1993, which spacecraft went missing whilst on a mission to Mars?

548. Which historic structure in Lucerne was destroyed by fire in 1993?

549. When King Baudouin of Belgium died on July 31 1993, who succeeded him?

550. Which event caused a former inmate of Treblinka to say: 'Gentlemen, now all the Nazis can celebrate'?

ENTERTAINMENT AND THE ARTS

1. Ferris. Ma Larkin's real life name is Pam Ferris; Rodney Bewes's character in the *Likely Lads* was Bob Ferris.

2. 526,000.

3. Gilbert Harding.

4. *Andy Pandy*.

5. The Daleks.

6. *Billy Bunter*. The school is Greyfriars.

7. Mr Pastry.

8. *Come Dancing*.

9. They all painted posters for the London Underground.

10. Librarian.

11. *1984* by George Orwell.

12. They were the films found in the bunker where Hitler died (or didn't die but substituted a double, depending on your liking for conspiracy theories).

13. John Malkovich.

14. In both cases another version of the story by another company was being filmed at the same time and both versions were released in the same year. *Robin Hood* starred Patrick Bergin and Ms Thurman; *Robin Hood, Prince of Thieves* starred Kevin Costner and Mary Mastroantonio. *Dangerous Liaisons* also had Ms Thurman in its cast whilst the rival version was called *Valmont*.

15. *Simply Ballroom*.

16. *Wilde Alliance*.

17. George Bernard Shaw.

18. Christopher Gable.

19. Maureen Lipman.

20. A S Byatt (Antonia Susan)

21. Peter Ackroyd.

22. Malcolm Bradbury.

23. Barry Took.

24. Shula, Kenton, David and Elizabeth.

25. Ambridge, Borsetshire.

26. *Trilby* by George Du Maurier.

27. R D Wingfield. David Jason.

28. *Today.*

29. *Woman's Hour.*

30. 1961.

31. *The Avengers.*

32. Richard Chamberlain.

33. 13. Six in 1975 and seven in 1979.

34. Jack Regan. George Carter.

35. *O.T.T.* (OVER THE TOP)

36. 1989.

37. Linda Hamilton.

38. Jennifer Jason Leigh.

39. Shakespeare.

40. Abelard and Heloise.

41. *Chariots of Fire.*

42. Vangelis.

43. Jeanine Deckers.
44. Stan Barstow.
45. Joss Ackland and Clare Bloom.
46. 'Amen' – last sentence in the whole book.
47. Lady Macbeth.
48. Kes, (by Barry Hines).
49. *Z for Zacchariah*.
50. Rita Mae Brown.
51. Robert.
52. Willibald.
53. *A Study in Scarlet*.
54. Sam Beeton, Mrs Beeton's husband.
55. Muriel Spark.
56. *A Sense of Guilt*.
57. Julie Covington.
58. Edward VIII and Mrs Simpson.
59. *Spare Rib*.
60. Thelma.
61. *Porridge*. *Auf Wiedersehen, Pet*.

62. Robert Robinson.
63. George Harrison.
64. *Abigail's Party.*
65. Timothy Dalton – later to be 007.
66. James Hazell.
67. Six.
68. F Murray Abraham.
69. *The Winslow Boy.*
70. *Glengarry Glen Ross.*
71. Mary Shelley.
72. *Jurassic Park.*
73. *Look Who's Talking.*
74. Himself.
75. She jumped to her death from the HOLLYWOOD sign.
76. Fatty Arbuckle.
77. They wrote standing up.
78. *Week Ending.*
79. Damien Hirst.
80. *The Messiah.*

81. John Adams.
82. René Magritte.
83. Six.
84. *Pictures at an Exhibition*.
85. Butterworth.
86. Glass design.
87. *Henry IV*.
88. Charles Rennie Mackintosh.
89. *The Scream*.
90. William Morris.
91. The Pre-Raphaelite Brotherhood.
92. Crystal Palace – it housed the Great Exhibition.
93. Both had sons who were kidnapped.
94. Mae West.
95. Trigger and Lassie.
96. *Midnight's Children*.
97. Rachel Whiteread.
98. Anne Aston.
99. Bill Bryson.

100. Alistair Cooke.

101. Kiri Te Kanawa.

102. Band of the Black Watch.

103. James Taylor.

104. *Working Girl.*

105. The Waltz.

106. Stephen Foster.

107. Geena Davis and Susan Sarandon.

108. *Dear John.*

109. Bart Simpson.

110. Helen Reddy.

111. Cable Network News.

112. Three.

113. Danny De Vito.

114. *Back to the Future.*

115. Delius.

116. James Woods.

117. Kenneth Branagh.

118. *84 Charing Cross Road.*

119. *Daughters of the American Revolution* (DAR)

120. Cor Anglais.

121. Edgar Allen Poe.

122. Pushkin.

123. Origins of words.

124. *The Colour Purple*.

125. Welsh.

126. *Desperately Seeking Susan*.

127. They were destroyed in a major fire at Universal Studios.

128. Kirk Douglas.

129. *Reservoir Dogs*. The other film that had colours for names was *The Taking of Pelham 1–2–3*.

130. Melanie Griffith.

131. Whoopi Goldberg.

132. James Dean.

133. The film was financed by Dodi Fayed, one of the brothers who own the store.

134. Colin Welland.

135. Johnny Weissmuller.

136. *Casablanca.*

137. *Butch Cassidy and the Sundance Kid.*

138. *Brief Encounter.*

139. She was married to Peter Fleming, the brother of Ian Fleming, creator of 007.

140. *The Hustler.*

141. Paul Newman and Strother Martin – in *Cool Hand Luke* he was the prison governor and in *Butch Cassidy and the Sundance Kid* he was the Bolivian miner the duo guarded on the way to the bank and back.

142. J R Ewing in *Dallas.*

143. George Peppard.

144. Warren Beatty.

145. Angie Dickinson.

146. Kirk Douglas.

147. Greta Garbo.

148. Jimmy Durante.

149. John Wayne.

150. Marx Brothers.

151. Jack Klugman and Tony Randall.

152. Bela Lugosi.

153. Australia.

154. England.

155. Sir Peter Ustinov.

156. Russia.

157. In a lift.

158. Babs Lord from Pan's People.

159. Jimmy Young.

160. Elvis Presley and Cliff Richard.

161. Stephane Grappelli, Django Reinhardt, Joseph Reinhardt, Pierre Ferret, Louis Vola, Tony Rovira, Eugene Vees, Emmanuel Soudieux, Roger Grassnet, Roger Chaput. (Yes, we know there are more than five but they all operated a sort of rota for performances and recordings.)

162. Clannad.

163. John Masefield.

164. Charlotte-Currer Bell; Emily-Ellis Bell; Anne-Acton Bell.

165. Michael Kitchen.

166. Lee Hazlewood.

167. Cilla Black.

168. *Howard's Way.*

169. Brighouse and Rastrick.

170. Chiffons.

171. 'He's So Fine'.

172. The Wombles.

173. *The Rivals*.

174. Jesus Christ.

175. Maya Angelou.

176. The Argonauts.

177. Long time ago. Long since. Long ago. (Accept any answer that approximates to any of these.)

178. Alan Ayckbourn.

179. Aphra Benn.

180. Luke.

181. 1611.

182. *The Cricket on the Hearth*.

183. Aleister Crowley.

184. Roald Dahl.

185. *A Dance to the Music of Time*.

186. *The Mystery of Edwin Drood*.

187. Edward Morgan.

188. Slaughter, Conquest, Famine and Death.
189. Henrik Ibsen.
190. Fourteen.
191. Mycroft.
192. Gerard Manley Hopkins.
193. A E Housman.
194. Stanley Kubrick.
195. Ira Levin.
196. St Mary Mead.
197. They were all Poet Laureate.
198. Seventeenth.
199. Ruritania.
200. Mythical swords.
201. The father of King Arthur.
202. Oscar Wilde.
203. Sir Christopher Wren.
204. Braque.
205. Craquelure.
206. Diptych.

207. Gobelins.

208. A jointed wooden figure used by artists to assist in their drawings of the human form. Also has been called a marionette and a manikin.

209. Silk screen printing.

210. Charles Tenniel.

211. Joseph Mallord William.

212. The Uffizi.

213. The Victoria and Albert.

214. Margery Allingham.

215. *Westward Ho.*

216. *The Rime of the Ancient Mariner.*

217. Athos, Porthos and Aramis. (D'Artagnan was a friend of the trio, not one of the Musketeers.)

218. Sylvia Plath.

219. He was E F Benson and wrote the Mapp and Lucia books.

220. Ambrose Bierce.

221. Eric Blair.

222. Gustave Flaubert.

223. Melvyn Bragg.

224. *Brideshead Revisited* by Evelyn Waugh.

225. *Catch 22.*
226. Eighteen.
227. Agatha Christie.
228. It was a circulating library.
229. John Clare.
230. The press.
231. Gandhi.
232. The Garrick.
233. A geographical index or dictionary.
234. Children's illustrations.
235. Nell Gwyn.
236. Patricia Highsmith.
237. 1926.
238. Incunabula or Incunables.
239. John Van Druten. It was a dramatisation based on Christopher Isherwood's *Goodbye to Berlin*.
240. Jane Eyre.
241. Jerome K. Jerome.
242. John Maynard Keynes.
243. He was a clergyman.
244. 1660 to 1669. (Accept any answer within two or three years of that.)

245. *Kubla Khan.*

246. The Nobel Prize for Literature.

247. Alison Lurie.

248. Daniel Eastermann.

249. Phileas Fogg. (Not Phineas as sometimes stated.)

250. John Le Carré.

251. Edward Lear.

252. Lady Caroline Lamb.

253. Magdalene College.

254. *The* (Manchester) *Guardian.*

255. Dame Ngaio Marsh.

256. *The Mill on the Floss.*

257. An alphabet of twenty characters used by the ancient British and Irish. (Accept alphabet.)

258. John Osborne.

259. Wilfred Owen.

260. Nicolo Paganini.

261. Jane Campion.

262. Terry Pratchett.

263. The first Sunday after Easter.

264. Arthur Ransome.

265. Sheila Delaney.

266. Saki.

267. Theology, Civil Law, Hebrew, Greek, Divinity, Physic, Medicine, Ecclesiastical History, Modern History, Moral and Pastoral Theology.

268. Vita Sackville-West.

269. *The Catcher in the Rye*.

270. *Les Misérables*.

271. Seventeenth. (1666 to be exact.)

272. The Turin Shroud.

273. Sari.

274. *Whatever Happened to Baby Jane?*

275. Mary Pickford.

276. Napoleon.

277. Ascoyne/D'Ascoyne.

278. *Sunset Boulevard*.

279. None.

280. Robert Donat.

281. *Liverpool Oratorio* by Paul McCartney and Carl Davies.

282. 'The rosy red cheeks of the little children' (From *England Swings* by Roger Miller.)

283. Walt Disney.

284. Elizabeth Butler.

285. Milton/Gummo.

286. John Creasey.

287. *Charley's Aunt.*

288. W C Fields.

289. Barrington Pheloung.

290. They were all the subjects for parts of Elgar's *Enigma Variations*.

291. He faked paintings by Dutch Old Masters especially Vermeer during the 1940s.

292. Babette.

293. Sexton Blake.

294. In the late 18th century it was claimed to be a long lost Shakespeare play but was actually forged by William Henry Ireland.

295. A Skye terrier who slept each night on his master's grave from 1858 to 1872. He was buried next to his master. The memorial to him consists of a drinking fountain for dogs with a bronze statue of Greyfriars Bobby.

296. Eva Peron in the film of the Lloyd-Webber musical *Evita*.

297. Hotspur in *Henry IV, Part 1*.

298. Robert Browning.

299. *Five Guys Named Moe.*

300. *Star Wars, The Empire Strikes Back* and *Return of the Jedi.*

301. Pride, avarice (or covetousness or greed), anger, envy, lust, gluttony, sloth.

302. Bill Medley and Bobby Hatfield.

303. Sarah Brightman and José Carreras.

304. Francis Ruffelle.

305. Edward Elgar.

306. Oceanus, Coius, Crius, Hyperion, Iapetus, Cronus, Thea, Rhea, Themis, Mnemosyne, Phoebe and Tethys.

307. Gioacchino Rossini.

308. Francois-Marie Arouet.

309. April 30. (Accept April or May.)

310. Fleetwood Mac's.

311. The pictures are produced of raised lines thus enabling the blind to 'see' the pictures.

312. *Cheers.*

313. Stewart Granger.

314. It is called *Scarlett* and the author is Alexander Ripley.

315. Père Lachaise cemetery.

316. Christopher Nolan.

317. *Phantom of the Opera*.

318. Frederick Ashton.

319. She sued them for a story alleging that she had an adulterous affair with Prince Andrew.

320. Alan Bennett.

321. Jack Pallance.

322. Derek Walcott.

323. Superman.

324. The Folies Bergère.

325. *Fidelio* by Beethoven.

326. *The Magic Flute* by Mozart.

327. Richard Chamberlain.

328. Liszt.

329. Half Voice.

330. Dashing, bold, with great spirit.

331. Twenty.

332. Liszt.

333. Italian.

334. Danish.

335. Edward Elgar.

336. William Walton.

337. Wagner.

338. Charles Ives.

339. The English Channel.

340. Sir Arthur Sullivan.

341. Mendelssohn.

342. 1685.

343. Philip Heseltine. He also wrote under the name of Rab Noolas (think about it!).

344. Pluto.

345. John Cage.

346. You would blow it – it was a 16th century bass cornet.

347. Chopin.

348. *A Village Romeo and Juliet* by Delius.

349. *Die Fledermaus*.

350. Leonard Bernstein.

351. Sir William Walton.

352. George Butterworth.

353. Charles Alkan.

354. Johann Maelzel.

355. Janáček.

356. Smetana.

357. Aubrey Beardsley.

358. Mary Evans.

359. Thomas Stearns.

360. 'A harmless drudge'?

361. David Hockney.

362. He decoded the hieroglyphics on the Rosetta Stone.

363. O Henry.

364. An eagle mistook Aeschylus' bald head for a rock and dropped the tortoise on it! (No, it doesn't sound very likely to us either, but that's what the tale says.)

365. Isaac Asimov.

366. Frankenstein – the four supposedly passed a week-end in Switzerland writing tales of the supernatural. Mary Wollstonecraft Shelley's was the only one ever published.

367. Clement Clarke Moore.

368. Three hundred.

369. Forty-eight. (Includes two that were in Germany during World War II that are now missing but presumed to be safe.)

370. Rossini.

371. The hurdy-gurdy.

372. It is one performed on horseback.

373. They both died on the same date – April 23rd 1616.

374. Playing cards.

375. Frank Sinatra.

376. *The Comedy of Errors*.

377. Dostoevsky.

378. He had no external ears.

379. George Byron.

380. It is a mythical beast.

381. The art of making prints from engraved wood. (Accept any reasonable variation of the answer.)

382. Disneyland.

383. EuroDisney.

384. He was created a CBE.

385. Toothpaste – Gibbs SR to be precise.

386. McGill – his first name was never known. (The actor was Richard Bradford.)

387. Boris Karloff.

388. Jack Webb.

389. *The Larkins.*

390. David Jacobs.

391. Patrick McGoohan. (So much for those who say the part of Bond always must go to someone British.)

392. *That Was The Week That Was.*

393. Clint Eastwood.

394. Keith Fordyce.

395. *Steptoe and Son.*

396. 'I'll give it five' as made famous on *Thank Your Lucky Stars* and not *Juke Box Jury*, as many people seem to think.

397. Fred.

398. Frank Marker.

399. Virgil, Scott, Alan, Gordon and John.

400. *Not Only, But Also.*

401. Micky Dolenz, Mike Nesmith, Davy Jones and Peter Tork.

402. *How.*

403. Lots of DIY. (Next time you're stuck in B&Q, you'll know who to blame.)

404. Johnny Morris.

405. *All Gas And Gaiters.*

406. Tara King, played by Linda Thorson.

407. Soames Forsyte.

408. John Alderton.

409. *The Power Game.*

410. Ashton.

411. They all began their careers as Butlins' redcoats.

412. *Take Three Girls.*

413. *The Persuaders.*

414. Sally Geeson.

415. *Budgie.*

416. Tim Brooke-Taylor, Graeme Garden, Bill Oddie.

417. Geoffrey Bubbles Bon Bon.

418. Nugent.

419. Bungle, Zippy and George.

420. Optional Reception of Announcements by Coded Line Electronics.

421. Princess Anne and Mark Phillips.

422. Linsey de Paul.

423. The Oxo family.

424. William Franklin.

425. Ridley Scott.

426. Annette Crosbie.

427. Margot, Jerry, Tom and Barbara.

428. Magnus Pyke.

429. Noel Edmonds.

430. Tom Baker.

431. Diane Keene.

432. Olivia Hussey.

433. *Going Straight.*

434. *Butterflies.* (Written by Carla Lane; starred Wendy Craig.)

435. Sandra. Her parents made occasional appearances in the series and were only ever referred to as Mr and Mrs Boswell.

436. Peter Egan.

437. Peter Bowles. (*To the Manor Born.*)

438. *Take The High Road.*

439. Castle Howard in Yorkshire.

440. Noelle Gordon.

441. Freeway.

442. The water storage tank at the top of the building was ruptured.

443. *The Reader's Digest.*

444. Tracy Lord.

445. *All Quiet on The Western Front* and *Elvira Madigan*.

446. Dudley Moore.

447. Jack Hargreaves.

448. It was the first programme to be shown on Channel Four.

449. Sam Neill.

450. David Frost, Michael Parkinson, Robert Kee, Angela Rippon and Anna Ford.

451. Ann, George(ina), Julian, Dick and Timmy the dog.

452. *The Bill*.

453. Colleen McCullough.

454. Bad Attitude.

455. Portugal. (She left to open a bar and restaurant).

456. Granville.

457. *Hot Metal*.

458. 1985.

459. John Thaw.

460. Jonathan Gash.

461. David Vine.

462. Beamish. (The actual beer promoted was Beamish stout but Morse only drank bitter).

463. Joey and Aveline.

464. *Crossroads.*

465. As the Gold Blend couple.

466. *A Very British Coup.*

467. Steve Guttenberg, Tom Selleck and Ted Danson.

468. Ringo Starr.

469. A dog, a cat and a mouse.

470. Inspector Wexford.

471. *Fraggle Rock.*

472. Reginald Perrin.

473. Judi Dench in *Behaving Badly.*

474. Grace Jones.

475. Jack Rosenthal.

476. Patrick Stewart.

477. Percy.

478. *I'm Sorry I Haven't A Clue.*

479. 'American Pie'.

480. 20,000.

481. They were all originally BBC radio series that made their way on to television.

482. *Eldorado.*

483. *GBH* by Alan Bleasdale.

484. *A Time To Dance.*

485. Bob, the alien spirit. (The show was *Twin Peaks* so the apparent answer might be a hoax!)

486. Squariel.

487. *Watching.*

488. Dustin Hoffman and Meryl Streep.

489. Gyles Brandreth.

490. Maureen Lipman.

491. Timothy Lumsden.

492. Prince Charles and Lady Diana's wedding.

493. Captain Frank Furillo.

494. Yosser Hughes played by Bernard Hill in *Boys From The Blackstuff.*

495. Cosgrove Hall.

496. *Big Deal.*

497. Two. *Robin's Nest* and *George and Mildred.*

498. Hannah Gordon. (The series was *Upstairs, Downstairs.*)

499. Elaine Stritch and Donald Sinden.

500. *South Bank Show.*

501. *The Old Grey Whistle Test.*

502. Film '94, (or any year.)

503. David Soul and Paul Michael Glaser.

504. Kojak.

505. They are made out of 'ticky-tacky'.

506. *Bye, Bye Birdie*.

507. He was the MC at the nightclub.

508. *Carrie*.

509. David Cassidy.

510. Abba.

511. Law.

512. Michael Crawford.

513. Jim Dale.

514. Kiki Dee – probably best known for her duet with Elton John 'Don't Go Breaking My Heart'.

515. Richard Gere.

516. Joyce Grenfell.

517. Noel Harrison, (son of Rex).

518. *Jeeves*. (Apparently it's a collaboration that both desperately try to forget).

519. Donny Osmond.

520. She married Haley Jr the son of the actor who played the Tin Man in the film.

521. *Crossroads*.

522. They have all expressed a desire to open the batting for England at Lords.

523. Tarrant.

524. The original books had Morse driving a Lancia but following the success of the television version this was changed in subsequent reprintings.

525. Ben Kingsley.

526. Gordon Honeycombe.

527. 'Decayed artists'. (Extensive litigation by his distant relatives meant that no 'decayed artist' received anything.)

528. Thomas Arne.

529. 'The Soldier'. (Rupert Brooke)

530. A(lan) A(lexander) Milne.

531. *Cruden's Concordance* – a guide to all the major words, proper names and place names in the Bible.

532. The Courtauld Collection, Courtauld Institute.

533. Correggio.

534. Copperplate.

535. James Fenimore Cooper.

536. No, not Madame DeFarge, Madame Tussaud.

537. The Stradivarius violin.

538. A glass eye – not the same one!

539. Dance marathons.

540. The Polka – as named from the Czech, Pulka.

541. They are the only two English novels to be included in the Vatican's list of banned books.

542. The world's first Juke Box.

543. The statue of Eros.

544. Mata Hari – literally it translates as 'eye of the day'.

545. William Shakespeare's.

546. Piano.

547. Andy Williams.

548. A tent maker.

549. Each has only one chapter.

550. *Assault on Precinct Thirteen.*

551. Marilyn Monroe.

552. Carrots.

553. Both were born in India.

554. Nothing but his name and dates. (Not 'on the whole I'd rather be in Philadelphia' – nor did he say this on his deathbed. His real dying words were '**** the whole world and every **** in it except you, Carlotta' – she being his long abiding girlfriend.)

555. All were raised as girls by wacky mothers. (In

Hemingway's case his elder sister Marceline was even held back for a year so the pair of them could enter school as twins. He ran away from home at fifteen. Wonder why?)

556. The Romans. Knowing that an army marched on its stomach, the Romans needed their own supplies to advance through hostile territory. The haggis was the closest thing to tinned food of the time.

557. Cabbage Patch Kids. (No accounting for taste, is there?)

558. Jaws.

559. 1948.

560. *The Matchmaker* by Thornton Wilder.

561. Schizophrenia.

562. Douglas Fairbanks.

563. Piccadilly Circus, (in 1896).

564. Tessie O'Shea.

565. The Goat and Compasses.

566. Mongooses.

567. 'Beam me up, Scotty!'

568. Cuneiform – from the Latin *cuneus*, a wedge.

569. Money – specifically a request for bribe money. (Don't ask what it means in Greece!)

570. Morris Dancing – the Moors. (It was originally a

sword dance of the Moorish warriors, the swords now replaced by little sticks with ribbons attached.)

571. Guardian Media Group.

572. Luciano Pavarotti, José Carreras and Placido Domingo.

573. *Groundhog Day.*

574. Rudyard Kipling.

575. $650,000.

576. Galileo.

577. A long wooden boat, believed to have been used for cross-channel voyages.

578. The Turkish sued the US for the return of these items which had been illegally excavated and exported. They won!

579. Frank Zappa.

580. William Powell and Myrna Loy.

581. Victoria Holt. (Also known as Jean Plaidy but born Eleanor Alice Hibbert.)

582. Billy Eckstine.

583. Les Dawson.

584. Lou Ferrigno. (Bill Bixby was the mild-mannered doctor who turned nasty when angry.)

585. Margaret, Duchess of Argyll.

586. Michael Crichton.

587. *Fly Fishing* by J R Hartley. So many people pestered bookshops asking for it that publishers Stanley Paul commissioned J R Hartley's *Memoirs*.

588. Edinburgh Fringe.

589. Liverpool – on the Albert Dock.

590. Two. It was published piecemeal from 1884 to 1928 and that was the edition in use until the second edition was published at the end of the 1980s. Incidentally, the whole twenty volume set was produced in America as was the *Encyclopaedia Britannica*.

591. Tom Hanks.

592. *The Shining*.

593. 1981. (Picasso died eight years previously.)

594. Lola Montez – real name Marie Gilbert. (King Louis I of Bavaria was so besotted with her that he created her a countess and allowed her to have increasing sway over the business of state. Her scheming eventually provoked a revolution.)

595. Bert Lahr.

596. The Battle of Jutland, (May 31 and June 1 1916).

597. The jigsaw puzzle.

598. Edith Piaf and Jean Cocteau.

599. Gordon Kaye, star of *Allo, Allo*. (He made a good recovery.)

600. Manchester.

601. Glasgow.

602. Roald Dahl.

603. Claus von Bulow.

604. It was the cost of the Newspaper Tax or, as the paper described it, the cost of the 'Taxes on Knowledge'.

605. They have all played God – Sutherland in *Johnny Got His Gun*, Burns in a whole series of *Oh, God* films and Richard Pryor in *In God We Trust* (1980).

606. P G Wodehouse.

607. Camberley.

608. London Broadcasting Company (LBC) and Capital Radio.

609. *Sesame Street*.

610. Aslan.

611. The Museum of the Moving Image.

612. Natalia Makarova.

613. 'What immortal hand or eye / Could frame thy fearful symmetry?' ('The Tiger' by William Blake).

614. Donald Duck.

615. Sir Arthur Bliss.

616. Bruce Springsteen.

617. *Clambake.*

618. 'Tubular Bells' by Mike Oldfield.

619. Arthur Koestler.

620. Mailer. Arthur Miller was the third and last husband of Marilyn Monroe.

621. Gloria Steinem.

622. Andy Warhol.

623. *The Threepenny Opera.*

624. The Cat and Fiddle.

625. Nobody knows. It was an unnamed servant summoned by Delilah, she did not do the job herself. To be really pedantic his head was shaved not shorn.

626. *Pravda* and *Izvestiya*. Pravda means truth; Izvestiya means news. In pre-collapsed Russia, they used to say there is no Pravda in Izvestiya and there's no Izvestiya in Pravda.

627. Joseph and his coat of many colours but the original text refer only to a garment with long sleeves.

628. Somnus. (Do not accept Morpheus – he was the son of Somnus and the god of dreams.)

629. Fleming's own mother – a gauleiter by all accounts. Throughout his childhood Fleming himself always addressed her as 'M'.

630. Alan B'Stard – The New Statesman.

631. Codpiece.

632. *Travels With A Donkey.*

633. *Kidnapped.*

634. Louis Armstrong.

635. Colonel Potter.

636. Liberace.

637. *The Owl and The Pussycat.*

638. Colour bar wouldn't allow them into the studios.

639. King Solomon.

640. A sheep.

641. Twenty-four.

642. The nine of diamonds – most likely for the nine lozenges on the coat of arms of the Earl of Stair and for his enthusiastic participation in the massacre at Glencoe.

643. Debra Winger.

644. Grinling Gibbons.

645. Sir Edwin Landseer.

646. Buonarroti.

647. John Ruskin.

648. None – nothing that is indisputably by him still survives. (Incidentally, many of the things he designed

were mere flights of fancy – many of his buildings and other structures would never have stood up or worked.)

649. Icon, from the Greek *eikon*, a likeness.

650. Sir Peter Paul Rubens.

SCIENCE, INDUSTRY AND TECHNOLOGY

1. Lanthanum.
2. Cobalt. From Kobold.
3. Titan.
4. Proteins.
5. Artificial intelligence.
6. Read Only Memory and Random Access Memory.
7. INTernational TELecommunications SATellite Organisation.
8. Ships. It is a method of ship construction where the dominant feature is longitudinal framing.
9. 70 million years. (Approx 215 to 145 million years ago.)

10. It is an instrument used in mine ventilation surveys to assess the cooling effect of air currents.
11. In the pancreas.
12. Launch-window or window of opportunity.
13. Birds – it is a form of botulism.
14. Laughing gas.
15. Monkey-tail.
16. Vitamin B – nicotinic acid/niacin.
17. Night blindness.
18. It is an alloy of copper and zinc, and sometimes tin.
19. A mechanical model of the solar system – it shows the relative motions of the planets. (Named after Charles Boyle, Earl of Orrery.)
20. Pangaea.
21. Rapid eye movement – a phase which occurs several times during sleep.
22. She was Typhoid Mary, an asymptomatic carrier who was responsible for at least ten outbreaks of the disease in New York.
23. It is the study of soil.
24. The nearest point to the Earth in the orbit of a spacecraft, missile etc.

25. Whooping cough.
26. Phobos and Deimos.
27. Io, Europa, Ganymede and Callisto.
28. Vulcan.
29. Stealth.
30. Seven.
31. Ada Lovelace.
32. Insects.
33. It is the stated period within each hour during which all marine transmissions must close down and listen on the international distress frequency.
34. 1645. It was actually invented in 1642.
35. 1815.
36. He was the first person to take off in an airplane from the deck of a ship (1910), thus proving that aircraft carriers are possible.
37. Du Pont.
38. They were originally trade names that have become generic terms.
39. Mark Twain.
40. Empire State Building.

41. Isaac Singer – first mass producer of a viable sewing machine.
42. DNA Structure.
43. Velcro.
44. Twenty-five.
45. Germany – in the 1920s.
46. Photocopier.
47. The safety razor.
48. The voice for the Speaking Clock service. (Incidentally, the voice was that of Jane Cain.)
49. Earl's Court – on 4 October 1911.
50. Video Recorder.
51. Volkswagen Beetle.
52. Wheel clamp – first introduced to Britain in 1983.
53. Sixteen.
54. Apothecary's weights.
55. 2,240.
56. 5½.
57. Old English coins.
58. 9,113.

59. A mile.

60. Paper.

61. Frustum.

62. Four.

63. Ibis.

64. A weapon of war designed to throw very heavy objects.

65. A craft that was successfully manoeuvred underwater. (Invented during the first quarter of the 17th century. Allow submarine.)

66. Edentata.

67. Very flat ocean-floor area.

68. The Pacific.

69. Newton's First Law of Motion.

70. Percival Lowell.

71. 12th. (By Peter of Colechurch in 1176.)

72. In the palace of Khorsabad near Nineveh. (Accept Assyria or Iraq.)

73. Benjamin Baker.

74. Galileo.

75. Ascanio Sobrero (in 1846).

76. Sand sea or shifting sand dune.
77. Des Moines, Iowa.
78. Gaston Plante.
79. A therapeutic technique which uses localized freezing to remove or destroy diseased tissue.
80. Padua and Pisa. (Established 1545).
81. William Harvey.
82. ABO blood groups were discovered in 1901.
83. Joseph and Etienne.
84. The science of the nature of man, or in its widest sense, mankind.
85. Sun-dried clay bricks, a structure built from those bricks or the clay soil from which those bricks are made. (Adobe is a Spanish word.)
86. Teflon.
87. British computers that cracked codes during the Second World War.
88. The first video game.
89. He developed another keyboard layout intended to reduce the amount of finger movement needed when typing.
90. Write Once Read Many – it is a Compact Disc that

can be written to by the user and is then generally used for archival purposes.

91. Very Large Scale Integration.

92. Central processing unit; arithmetic and logic unit; disk operating system; computer aided/assisted design; computer aided/assisted learning; windows, icons, mouse and pull-down menus; what you see is what you get.

93. Energy supply; water supply; construction.

94. 16 million. (Accept a million either side.)

95. Hydrogen; Helium.

96. John T Scopes.

97. Parkinson's disease.

98. Mulberry.

99. Vitamin B1.

100. A spring driven pocket watch – the first pocket watch ever made.

101. King Charles II (in 1675).

102. Isaac Newton.

103. It was awarded because the mouse had been genetically engineered.

104. Butterflies.

105. Silkworms. (It is a fungus.)

106. A rooster and a duck.

107. Nicholas Appert.

108. Carbon 14 dating.

109. Charles Dawson.

110. 90%.

111. Fifteen.

112. Challenger.

113. Great white shark.

114. Piezoelectricity.

115. Cocoa. (Accept chocolate.)

116. Percy Shaw, inventor of the cat's eye.

117. Foil milk bottle top.

118. Airfix.

119. Trivial Pursuit.

120. TCP.

121. Twenty-seven.

122. Edward I.

123. An orb and cross.

124. Four.

125. Redwing.

126. Monkey puzzle.

127. E621.

128. Edinburgh Castle – it is a 15th century bombard (cannon) weighing five tons.

129. Seven miles/eleven kilometres.

130. Lancewood.

131. 1939 – Polish cavalrymen charged German armoured columns. (Accept Second World War.)

132. Speaking in tongues.

133. It actually began in 1300, so accept 13th or 14th century.

134. Copper and zinc. (Half a mark for either.)

135. Hardness of gemstones.

136. Pearl.

137. Dandelion.

138. Charles Darwin.

139. International date-line.

140. Davenport.

141. A beat or stroke which stops 'dead' without recoil.

142. Death; its phenomena and causes. (Also can be the study of effects of death on family.)

143. Patrick Moore.

144. Study of public elections. (Can also be the study of voting trends.)

145. A system of electronic navigation developed during the Second World War.

146. Delft.

147. Shoulder. (Accept upper back or arm.)

148. Structure of the human population, particularly migration, birth and deaths.

149. Trees.

150. Cannabis fibre.

151. They were the two miners who met at the half way point in the Channel Tunnel.

152. A bird.

153. Derrick.

154. A mushroom. (Accept fungus.)

155. Horizontal moulding supported by pillars.

156. Typhoid.

157. A table giving the position of one or more celestial bodies.

158. Epoch.

159. Diamonds.

160. The amount of evaporation from a moist surface.

161. An experimental submarine powered by hydrogen peroxide – developed by the British during the Second World War.

162. Benjamin Franklin.

163. Channel and Greenwich.

164. York.

165. Thomas Cook.

166. Magnus Volk.

167. A railway sleeper.

168. London, Midland and Scottish; London and North Eastern; The Great Western and the Southern.

169. Amplitude Modulation and Frequency Modulation.

170. The practice of drilling a small hole in the skull.

171. British Thermal Unit.

172. August 1962. (A research scientist at Porton Down.)

173. Leprosy.

174. The largest gold nugget ever – it was called the Welcome Stranger.

175. Pierre and Marie Curie – the extraction of radium.

176. Six months – in Paris.

177. The Statue of Liberty.

178. Andrew Carnegie.

179. Gadolinium.

180. Erbium, Yttrium, Ytterbium, Terbium – all are named after Ytterby.

181. Organic compounds contain carbon, inorganic ones don't.

182. Louis Pasteur – he cured the silkworms of their parasites and so increased production.

183. One.

184. Potato.

185. One billionth of a meter.

186. Twelve thousand.

187. Twenty-four.

188. Jacques Cousteau.

189. He was his first cousin.

190. Pietro Angelo Secchi.

191. Alexander Graham Bell.

192. Two inches – dwarf willows on Greenland's tundra.

193. One flown by pedal power – it was called the

Gossamer Albatross and weighed seventy pounds.

194. Two.

195. 86 degrees Fahrenheit. It will melt in your hand.

196. Hiram Maxim, in 1884.

197. General Agreement on Tariffs and Trade.

198. Cats.

199. Woodrow Wilson.

200. The Andromeda galaxy.

201. Tycho Brahe.

202. 100 billion.

203. It was the first attempt to detect intelligent life in another world. (It was conducted in 1960 at the radio telescope at Green Bank, England.)

204. Nosebleed.

205. Robert William Thomson took out the patent in 1845.

206. Tit or titmouse.

207. Tortoiseshell.

208. Jethro Tull.

209. Turnbuckle.

210. In the ear.

211. Vanadium. (The name of the Goddess is Vanadis.)

212. It was a form of immunization. (Accept vaccination or inoculation.)

213. They are near the taste buds at the back of the tongue.

214. W.

215. Warble fly.

216. October 1992.

217. An area devoted to the culture of trees and woody plants.

218. It is a zoological term for dart-shaped.

219. It is the mineral cinnabar.

220. It is a variety of quartz but is sometimes called false topaz.

221. Doldrums.

222. Arachnid.

223. Anthrax.

224. About a pint.

225. Hurricane Andrew.

226. A baboon.

227. A Mercedes.

228. Bugatti.

229. Coade Stone.

230. PARallax SECond.

231. Thirteen.

232. The Bristlecone Pine. (The oldest specimen is over 4,900 years old which is quite a lot older than that other long lived tree, the sequoia.)

233. The borzoi.

234. It is a small deer.

235. Cabriolet.

236. A bell tower.

237. Cloister.

238. The Crux (Southern Cross) constellation.

239. It is dedicated to producing a complete map of human genetic make-up.

240. Blue or Violet.

241. Aspirin.

242. He was killed when a MIG jet crashed during a routine training flight.

243. 6000 degrees Fahrenheit/3300 degrees Celsius.

244. Aconite.

245. Clipper.

246. A wind, (produced by descending air currents on

the lee side of mountains – given its name because it came from the direction of Chinook Indian camp at the mouth of the Colombia River).

247. Another three hours. It stays above the horizon for around nineteen hours. (Accept any answer from two to four hours.)

248. Starts June 1 and finishes August 31.

249. It's in the constellation of Taurus.

250. From the intestine of the sperm whale.

251. An anchor.

252. Euston Arch – it stood outside the station until it was modernised.

253. Yellow/orange.

254. A small buffalo.

255. Aspartame.

256. 115 million gallons. (Accept any answer between 100 and 130 million gallons.)

257. Royal Geographical Society.

258. Centigrade to Fahrenheit.

259. Calorie.

260. Ductile.

261. Temperature. It has been superseded by centigrade.

262. Blackbody.

263. The 19th century.

264. They both are used to raise tender plants but a conservatory is attached to the main house whereas a greenhouse is situated in the working part of the garden.

265. A parrot.

266. Opals.

267. Coronagraph.

268. Six and twenty.

269. Destroyer, cruiser, battleship.

270. Southern Cross/Crux Constellation.

271. Cyanosis.

272. Amelia Earhart.

273. Twelve.

274. It is the name for the small holes in the walls of a castle through which missiles and liquid could be jettisoned.

275. Crocus.

276. 7 feet and ¼ inch. (Accept any answer within 6 inches.)

277. An imitation of marble.

278. The 1880s. (The quake of 1884.)

279. It measures pressure by the rate of dissipation of heat.

280. Radium, uranium and polonium, this last element being named after Marie Curie's native Poland.

281. Burroughs-Wellcome Pharmaceuticals. They were the first to produce swallow-friendly sized tablets and called the range Tabloid. (The new 'condensed' newspapers of the early twentieth century hi-jacked the term.)

282. Belgium.

283. It contains no mustard and it is not a gas but an atomised liquid.

284. 2/6d – two and sixpenny note, (that's twelve and a half pence. They were issued in 1941 in an attempt to conserve metal for the war effort and if you find one now it's worth about two grand – that's inflation for you!)

285. Dormouse. There are no others; not even the squirrel is a hibernator.

286. The Belfry. (Nothing to do with bells at all but based instead on the middle English 'berfray', a siege tower. The similarity in shape to a church spire caused the shift and the erroneous association with bells changed the spelling.)

287. The fox – the term is basically the Latin for

fox-mange which was anciently pandemic in Italy resulting in lots of little bald foxes running around the place.

288. 1903.

289. The United States. US tourists also spend the most on their travels abroad.

290. 33 million.

291. In Vietnam – the animal is similar to a cow but has a coat like a horse and horns like an antelope. It is named Vu Quang ox.

292. 15 million.

293. Endeavour.

294. Poland.

295. HOTOL. (Horizontal Take Off and Landing.)

296. Three years.

297. Bergamot.

298. Kiwi fruit.

299. King Charles spaniel.

300. Joshua Tree.

301. Benzine.

302. EPNS. (Electro plated nickel silver.)

303. The Guinea coin. The coin had not been produced since around 1800 but a special minting was carried

out to pay British forces. The coin is rare, known as the 'military' guinea and much sought after by collectors.

304. Six. (Accept an answer between five and seven.)

305. Misti.

306. Millefiori.

307. It is a fish – it has rows of luminous organs on its undersurface.

308. Cowslip.

309. A heart. Although they are not successful in the longer term, they are used as an in between measure for patients awaiting a full transplant.

310. Chlorofluorocarbon.

311. It was a weather satellite launched in April 1960.

312. A pulsar.

313. They were amongst the first twenty-three commercials to be screened on the night of September 22 1955 in the first independent television broadcasts in the UK. (If you wish to know what the others were: Batchelor's peas, Summer County margarine, Ekco radio and television sets, Oxo, Watney's, Kraft Cheese, Woman magazine, Coty, Remington Rand, Dunlop tyres, Cadbury's chocolate, Crompton bulbs, Lux soap, National Benzole, Surf, Gibbs S R, Brown and Polson, Ford and the Express Dairy company.)

314. The automatic telephone exchange. The wife of his major competitor was the supervisor at the old manual installation and all the girls were on a kickback for business calls diverted to her husband's establishment. After telling distraught callers that Strowger's line was busy, they advised them to try the other number.

315. She was the first person to be cremated – nothing terribly sophisticated, they simply threw wood and combustible oils on top of her body in the open grave at St George's cemetery in London's Hanover Square.

316. The parking meter.

317. The first public toilets, (the original cottage industry!).

318. Eros.

319. Kleenex tissues.

320. Banana. It does not grow on a tree and that which appears to be the trunk is a column of overlapped leaves. The 'fruit' is but the seed pod and the whole shooting match is secured underground by a rhizome not a network of roots. It is thus a herb.

321. Peanut – it grows underground and is actually part of the vegetable family.

322. Artichoke.

323. Rubies. (Diamonds are as common as muck – they

are dug out of the ground in their millions every year, industry takes most and the cost of those in the jewellery market is not generated by their rarity but by the difficulty in cutting and polishing.)

324. A ton of coal. In the terminology of flock merchants (feather merchants) seventeen hundredweight constitutes a ton. (Other odd 'tons' include herring – a ton of which is six thousand fish no matter what they weigh; and grain which can weigh in at as little as ten hundredweight per ton.)

325. The factor of seven is a myth. Dogs are reproducing after a year and fully matured by two. You count the first year as fifteen, the second year as ten and all subsequent years as five.

326. Seventy-two hours.

327. Forty-eight hours.

328. Water.

329. Seventy.

330. Fifty percent.

331. One gallon.

332. Sir Francis Bacon.

333. Bazooka – loosely based on the Dutch *bazuin*, a trumpet.

334. The water-bed.

335. Prophylactic.

336. Luna I.

337. 1920s.

338. Howard Carter and Lord Caernarvon.

339. New Zealander.

340. It decides on the legality of captures of goods and vessels at sea.

341. From 1952 to 1969.

342. He worked as an industrialist in the family firm – a flour making business known today as Rank Hovis Macdougall.

343. Colour blindness.

344. Red

345. Sartorius.

346. It is in Casablanca and was dedicated in August 1993 by King Hassan of Morocco. The laser beam is aimed at the Holy city of Mecca in Saudi Arabia.

347. Rolls Royce.

348. Quarter of a million years ago.

349. Vladimir Nabokov.

350. Joseph Rowntree.

351. They were all winners of the first ever Nobel Prizes.

352. Holland I.

353. One dollar.

354. Oil – he was in Persia.

355. The *Lucania* – the ship was in the Atlantic at the time.

356. Duck egg blue.

357. Belfast.

358. Sixty-five percent.

359. It is a coin – a Saudi Arabian coin. (There are twenty to the rial.)

360. The hologram.

361. The North Star.

362. In sea water – it floats in suspension in minute particles and there are literally millions of tons of it just bobbing about waiting to be extracted.

363. 380 miles. (Allow thirty miles each way.)

364. You would have red hair.

365. Limestone.

366. Colorado.

367. Seven.

368. Jupiter.

369. Sirius or the Dog Star.

370. 1978.

371. The number of molecules in 18 grams of water. (If it matters this is 602,000,000,000,000,000,000. Amedio Avogadro – Italian physicist – must have got pretty bored in 1842 when he actually sat down and worked this out!)

372. They used it to produce ink.

373. The blue whale.

374. The transistor.

375. Pluto. (Certainly no place to strike a match!)

376. Quinine. (The gin and tonic so popular with the British in India was born as a pleasant way to take one's medicine. Although now called tonic waters they were known in the last century as quinine waters, each bottle containing a daily dose.)

377. Id, Ego and Super Ego.

378. Haemophilia.

379. Sugar.

380. Uranus, (however you wish to pronounce it!).

381. The Big Dipper.

382. Vacuum cleaner.

383. The existence of Neptune.

384. On the eyelids.

385. Capillaries.

386. Shrews.

387. Russia.

388. Emerald.

389. Communications.

390. Bacteria – he pulled some half-digested food out of his mouth and pushed it under his home-made microscope.

391. Bloodroot.

392. William Bickford.

393. China.

394. 100 mph.

395. Stephen Babcock.

396. Carbon Dioxide.

397. Smell.

398. 1969.

399. The grape.

400. Five.

401. One byte.

402. An emerald.

403. 1976.

404. René Descartes.

405. Eighty-eight.

406. 248.

407. Six days.

408. The atom.

409. Mir.

410. Factor.

411. The cell.

412. 750. (Allow within fifty either side.)

413. Dice – when talking of his quantum theory Einstein made the observation 'God does not play dice'.

414. Copernicus. (In his native Polish his name means Little-Onion.)

415. Mercury.

416. The skin.

417. Twenty-eight.

418. Skin ulcers.

419. It has been observed to mate anything up to three hundred times an hour.

420. Twenty-two.

421. Scorpions.

422. The aorta.

423. Robert Oppenheimer; Project Manhattan.

424. Aspartame. (Canderel, Nutrasweet.)

425. The ears.

426. 17 feet. Accept any answer within a couple of feet.

427. The Dow Jones index – Charles Henry Dow was the first to devise the idea of charting general trends in stocks and shares prices.

428. Urbain Leverrier.

429. Buick and Oldsmobile.

430. 1900.

431. Sally Ride.

432. The Model A.

433. New Jersey.

434. Five. (From May 3 1951 onwards.)

435. St Peter's Basilica.

436. F W Woolworth. It was the first of the chain of stores which bear his name even today.

437. Cryogenics. It undertakes to 'freeze' people in the hope that one day a cure will be found for the illnesses that afflicted the person in life.

438. None. The oath lapsed years ago.

439. Ten.

440. The toad.

441. Pepsi. ('Come alive you're in the Pepsi generation'.)

442. Will o' the Wisp. It is marsh gas under spontaneous combustion which plays dancing flame at night across such terrain.

443. Almonds and cashews.

444. Formic acid.

445. Slave.

446. Insects.

447. The shopping trolley. He died in 1984 leaving a four hundred million dollar fortune (– but no one could push the coffin straight up the aisle!).

448. Contact lenses. Stanley was leaving the opticians with his owners in Bilbao and walked straight under a bus and was killed.

449. Coca-Cola.

450. Bar codes.

451. China.

452. 'Come here, Watson, I want you', (what happened next is perhaps best left to the imagination!).

453. Half tester.

454. The arterial system – the 'I' got lost (i.e. airterial.)

455. The yacht – from the German *jagen*. (Its shallow draft and speed made it a great favourite with pirates who hunted merchantmen on the high seas.)

456. Franz Anton Mesmer.

457. Australia.

458. Baked beans – there is no escape for the result!

459. The sun.

460. The llama.

461. Four.

462. A chevron, from the French *chevre*, a goat. (A pair of flying buttresses were thought to resemble goats reared up in combat.)

463. The opossum. (Do not accept possum, this is a separate creature living in Australia and not found anywhere in the US.)

464. Letters for the state of the hull, numbers for the ship's gear.

465. Typhoid.

466. Hailstones.

467. 1699 at Eddystone Rock. (Allow 25 years either way.)

468. Air Registration Board.

469. Malaria.

470. 1905.

471. Four miles an hour, each vehicle requiring three attendants, one of whom had to walk in front with a

red flag. (This was only intended for traction engines and was never applied to motor vehicles when they arrived.)

472. The Mary Rose was lifted from the sea bed, off Portsmouth, having sunk there in 1545.

473. Yes, John Dalton. (That was a trick question!)

474. 1518.

475. The first knitting machine.

476. 1594.

477. Snuff. The practised snuff sniffer never sneezed and only did so deliberately to indicate boredom politely. (Hence things of merit were 'not to be sneezed at'.)

478. 1985 – in January to be precise, a bit too cold.

479. CAT Scanner.

480. In the head. It is an air-containing cavity in the maxilla which communicates with the nasal cavity.

481. Aquifer.

482. Break down voltage.

483. The act of swallowing.

484. Fan-shaped.

485. Saturn.

486. It is an animated diagram which indicates the state

of operations by coloured lights, recorders or instruments – typically found in the control room of a process plant or electrical network.

487. A simplified parachute used for dropping supplies.

488. *The Great Egg Race* – a programme which challenged teams of inventors to come up with various Heath Robinson devices.

489. The mini-skirt.

490. Barbie doll.

491. Hula Hoops. (If contested, the Frisbee was launched by the same company in 1957).

492. Stevenson with his 'Rocket', which just touched 30 mph.

493. Charles Darwin on HMS *Beagle*.

494. The Tsarist family filmed with Queen Victoria at Balmoral.

495. Manchester Ship Canal.

496. Brunel's *Great Eastern* which, at 18,900 tons sported three times the displacement of any other ship afloat.

497. Henry Bessemer.

498. 1953 and it came in from France.

499. WC Roentgen.

500. The teddy bear, after Theodore Roosevelt.

501. Jacques Cartier who capitalised on his new found fame and opened a store on New Bond Street.

502. Crocodiles and alligators.

503. Turkish Bath.

504. The skin.

505. The mile-a-minute plant.

506. Twelve months.

507. An electric chair. (One of three he had ordered from America intending to bring his country the benefits of the twentieth century; but when it was pointed out to the dotty monarch that his country had no electricity, he scrapped two and had one upholstered for his imperial throne.)

508. The Evening Star.

509. 106.

510. Watling Street.

511. Germany – approximately 2,200 varieties.

512. Chicken and leeks.

513. Edward VII.

514. The turkey.

515. 1977.

516. The blood system.

517. The human body.

518. The jellyfish.

519. Seventy. (Allow within twenty either side.)

520. Sheffield.

521. Six – the centre squares on each face.

522. He was the first 'successful' heart transplant patient of Christian Barnard, and survived the operation by that number of days.

523. 405.

524. The laughing jackass.

525. That of the yak.

526. Wavelengths of light.

527. It is the densest element.

528. Per Lindstrand.

529. Monsoon.

530. Cats.

531. Fifteen years.

532. Russia – Luna 2 dropped a payload of miniature flags on to the surface of the moon in 1959 almost exactly ten years before the Americans actually landed a man there.

533. You would have no sense of smell.

534. 29½ million tons. (Accept any answer within 10 million tons either way.)

535. A type of calculator.

536. Tyne.

537. Places of equal cloud cover.

538. In the ocean; the Mid Ocean ridge extends for around 50 thousand kilometres.

539. Through their skin.

540. Aspic, (as named after the asp, the jelly being cold and slimy as people mistakenly believe the snake's skin to be; but it is of course quite dry.)

541. Both soups are served cold.

542. Vega.

543. CS gas.

544. Perfume or fragrance.

545. The Moon. Everything else is just man-made space junk.

546. She was the first person to die of radiation poisoning.

547. To four thousand metres.

548. A bind.

549. England, Northern Ireland, Wales, Scotland, Jersey, Guernsey and the Isle of Man.

550. Eight inches.

SPORT AND LEISURE

1. Fifty-eight. (Allow five years either side.)
2. Kirk Stevens – snooker player.
3. Vinny Jones.
4. Bram Stoker – author of *Dracula*.
5. Derbyshire, Gloucestershire, Kent, Lancashire, Middlesex, Nottinghamshire, Surrey, Sussex and Yorkshire.
6. Anne Boleyn.
7. Willie John McBride.
8. Zola Budd and Mary Dekker (Slaney).
9. Maricica Puica.
10. Betty Stove.

11. Rugby League.
12. Rachel Heyhoe-Flint.
13. Princess Anne.
14. Newmarket.
15. Lee Trevino.
16. Emily Davidson.
17. Jesse Owens.
18. Newton Heath.
19. Rotherham United.
20. Eighteen characters including spaces.
21. 1900–1910. Actual date 1906.
22. Winston Churchill.
23. Terry Marsh.
24. Aberdeen.
25. £5,500,000.
26. Trevor Francis, Steve Daley, Andy Gray.
27. Ingrid Kristiansen.
28. Henry Cooper.
29. James E Sullivan Award.

30. In the 1970s. (1977, to be exact.)

31. New York.

32. 48 kilogrammes; 105 pounds.

33. USA.

34. Grand Stand.

35. W G Grace's mother.

36. Royal Burgess Golfing Society of Edinburgh.

37. Wimbledon.

38. The Derby and The Oaks.

39. Ice Hockey.

40. Margaret Court.

41. John McEnroe.

42. It was discontinued after the 1924 games and reinstated in 1988.

43. Snooker/billiards/pool.

44. F A Cup.

45. Giacomo Agostini.

46. Yamaha.

47. Ferrari.

48. Mark Spitz – 7 medals in the 1972 Olympics.

49. Real Tennis.
50. Stephen Hendry.
51. Headbutting an official.
52. Cliff Thorburn.
53. Heather McKay.
54. Swimming (2.4 miles), cycling (112 miles), and a full marathon.
55. Basketball.
56. Tug-of-War.
57. 1933.
58. Foil, epée and sabre.
59. She was the first woman to swim the English Channel.
60. In the 1920s. (1927.)
61. May. (It runs until October.)
62. Five.
63. Sir Gordon Richards.
64. Eighteen a side.
65. Abner Doubleday.
66. Women golfers.

67. Lacrosse.

68. Stockport.

69. Fencing, swimming, pistol shooting, cross country running and riding.

70. Fifteen.

71. Bridge.

72. BBC Floodlit Trophy.

73. Nottingham Forest.

74. Because they were the same colours as the Argentinian strip.

75. Queen's Park Rangers.

76. 1930s. (1937.)

77. Chester.

78. Jochen Rindt. (Killed at practice at Monza in 1970 but already so far ahead in the points table that he won anyway.)

79. 1907.

80. Jenny Pitman.

81. Antwerp, 1920.

82. 4 ½ inches, 10.8 cm.

83. Baseball and badminton.

84. Twenty-five. (Allow any answer within five of correct answer.)

85. Matthew Pinsent, Stephen Redgrave.

86. Bows are regulated according to drawing strength.

87. They stopped to help their opponents in a canoeing contest when the opponents had trouble with their rudder. Once they had sorted out the problem, the race continued.

88. In the 1970s.

89. 1972.

90. Yachting, shooting and equestrian events.

91. Javelin, discus, jumping, running and wrestling.

92. Clay.

93. A fee, as well as the usual commemorative medal.

94. In-fighting.

95. Twelve.

96. Joe Louis.

97. Norman Selby.

98. James Dean.

99. Hungary.

100. John Gully

101. Greece. They were issued to coincide with the 1896 Olympic Games.

102. Forty-two. He said he did it for all senior citizens everywhere!

103. Trevor Berbick.

104. Italy.

105. They were raising money to ensure the Grand National could carry on.

106. They are the three thoroughbreds from whom all thoroughbred racehorses can trace their parentage.

107. January 1.

108. Geraldine Rees.

109. Boxing.

110. Thirty-eight inches.

111. Between 5.5 and 5.75 ounces.

112. Peter, the Lord's cat. He had an entry in the 1965 Wisden's.

113. In-swinger.

114. Curator.

115. It is a dog-sled race – first run in 1973.

116. Five.

117. 2,500 miles, 4,000 kilometres.

118. August 1992.

119. Eighteen.

120. Twelve.

121. The adipose fin has been removed.

122. It is a chair, usually with a harness, fastened to the deck at the stern of a fishing boat from which the big game sea angler tackles his catch.

123. 1961.

124. Birmingham (Small Heath).

125. Once.

126. Eight.

127. Eight.

128. Lori McNeil.

129. All England Lawn Tennis and Croquet Club.

130. Twelve.

131. Little Mo – Maureen Connolly.

132. Scrabble.

133. Pithian games.

134. Lotus-Ford.

135. 1912.

136. 1968.

137. Baltimore.

138. He refused to serve in the army during the Vietnam War.

139. A ball lying between your ball and the hole.

140. David Platt.

141. He was suffering from stress.

142. East Fife, East Sterling and Queen of the South.

143. The fine was increased to £1.5 million. The points penalty given was reduced to zero from the previous twelve.

144. Leroy Burrell.

145. Pete Sampras and Conchita Martinez.

146. England.

147. 16th century. (Actual date 1538, author Nicholas Wynmann, a professor of languages.)

148. She was competing in Hamburg.

149. Nine.

150. Polo – they competed for the Queens Cup at Guards Polo Club.

151. Coronation Cup, Eclipse Stakes and King George VI and Queen Elizabeth Diamond Stakes.

152. Eight: sprint, individual pursuit, kilometre time trial, 40-km points, team pursuit, keirin, motor paced, tandem sprint. (Accept any answer between six and ten.)

153. Zimbabwe.

154. Bridge.

155. Anatoly Karpov and Jan Timman.

156. Lennox Lewis. Riddick Bowe had refused to defend his title against Lewis and fought Holyfield instead. WBC awarded Lewis the title almost by default.

157. A parachutist descended on the ring during the seventh round.

158. Ronnie O'Sullivan – when he defeated Ian Hendry in the UK Championships.

159. Pocket billiards.

160. Lola-Ford Cosworth.

161. 239.14 kph/149.37 mph.

162. World Gliding Championships.

163. A two balloon craft in which Larry Newman attempted a round the world helium filled balloon flight (1993).

164. Eleven years old. She was accompanied by her flying instructor but did all the flying and navigating herself.

165. Don Bradman.

166. Water Polo. The six feet is measured from its height above the surface of the water.

167. Cricket. The 'obituary' notice appeared after England had lost to Australia, the last lines of the notice read: 'NB – The body will be cremated and the ashes taken to Australia'. The following year England beat the Australians who carried on the joke by providing some real ashes for the victorious team; hence the Ashes which have been contested ever since.

168. A rink.

169. Sir George Alfred Julius invented the automatic totalizator (tote).

170. Table tennis.

171. 1968 – October 6.

172. It was the England v West Germany match.

173. Cameroon.

174. Maiden.

175. Earvin.

176. Zina Garrison.

177. David Icke.

178. Steeplechase.

179. Six.

180. Curling.

181. 1875.

182. Shotgun.

183. Nordic and Alpine.

184. About five metres long and it is made from a fir tree.

185. Fencing.

186. Nine.

187. A competition toboggan.

188. The American rodeo – this is when the cowboy has to leap from horseback and wrestle a running steer and bring it to the ground.

189. Rowing.

190. Sky diving.

191. Falconry – it became easier to shoot the birds out of the sky.

192. Crossbow target shooting.

193. Fox hunting

194. The 18th century after Mont Blanc was first successfully climbed in 1786.

195. Kendo.

196. Aikido and Judo.

197. Wrestling.

198. Barry Sheene.

199. Joe Louis. (If they had had Lindbergh in the film they could have called it the Spirit of St Louis!)

200. *Octopussy*.

201. Clara Bow – otherwise known as the IT girl.

202. Peter Sellers. (Eat your heart out, Kato!)

203. Rossano Brazzi. He piled into the bulldozer in the opening sequence of *The Italian Job*.

204. Mr John (Blue Rinse) Forsyth of Dynasty. (He is also a horse racing fanatic with a stable of fifteen winners.)

205. Figure skating.

206. The upshot.

207. Dominoes – as named from the domino mask so favoured by Harlequin. (In turn the mask took its name from the Latin *dominus* – a lord or the lord. Since the mask was derived from the face screen once used by monks to keep them warm whilst wandering around in the winter, all you could see

were the white eyes against the cloth – just like the tiles.)

208. Its sprint speed over the quarter mile race.

209. Sixteen.

210. Orange.

211. Snooker. (It was a blend of pyramids and billiards and so named because in military slang a snooker was a snot-nosed recruit or cadet at Officer Training and, since all players at the new game were raw, they called it snooker.)

212. Racket – as based on the Arabic *rahat*. (As people's hands got sore, they adopted gloves which gradually became dished and made of stiffened leather which later had tensioned strings placed across to allow power shots.)

213. Royal – it was a variant of the game played by the nobility in castle courts, hence the name for the playing area in tennis today.

214. Cribbage – you turn the corner at the top of the board for the home run; the rows of peg holes were known as 'streets' so if your opponent was a long way behind he was 'not in the same street' as you and the game was finished (or dead) when somebody pegged out).

215. Greyhound (but accept lurcher – their only use was to bring down the King's deer).

216. Walter Matthau.

217. The line was uttered by Joe Jacobs, ironically the Jewish manager of the German fighter Max Schmelling, after Jack Sharkey had pounded his opponent into the canvas. Schmelling didn't do much better when he met Joe Louis.

218. Johnny Weissmuller.

219. Boxing is the most popular with 199 films to date and weightlifting is the least popular with a resounding one.

220. Robert Stack – Eliot Ness in *The Untouchables* where he never managed to shoot Frank Nitti!

221. Carousel.

222. Lacrosse.

223. Brooklands.

224. Dominoes or cribbage. Those who can't take their turn, or wish to capitulate, traditionally knock on the underneath of the table.

225. 'Two-six-heave'. (Tug-of-war was traditionally exercised on board British Navy fighting ships – sensible stuff given the restriction of space. Numbers two and six on a gun crew were responsible for hauling the cannon to and fro the port for loading, hence the odd numbers.)

226. Leader.

227. Live hare coursing – 'So Ho!' (Is that the sport's equivalent of 'Tally Ho'?)

228. Thirty minutes.
229. 10 metres; the women run 100 metres, the men 110 metres.
230. Withdraw – as both parties must withdraw from the game and start again.
231. 2¼ miles.
232. Maxine Juster.
233. Deafness in one ear after heading the ball.
234. Muhammed Ali was stripped of his title for draft dodging and refused to compete.
235. Graeme Obree.
236. Dallas Cowboys and Detroit Lions.
237. He cycled in Bordeaux, France.
238. Ambrose Lighthouse in New York Harbour and Lizzard Point in the English Channel.
239. Women competed for the first time.
240. The US Open.
241. Jogging. (Ironically, he died whilst running.)
242. Ally McLeod.
243. Leon Spinks.
244. 1980.
245. Nadia Comaneci.

246. David Wilkie.

247. Denis Howell.

248. Lasse Viren.

249. A group of protesters seeking the release of a prisoner dug up the pitch.

250. John Conteh. (The previous British holder was Freddie Mills.)

251. Nick Price.

252. Jan Kodes.

253. Two hundred feet.

254. Formula Three.

255. 'Black' Jack.

256. The Fastnet Race. Fifteen sailors died, only 177 of the 306 yachts that started actually finished the course.

257. *British Steel.*

258. Uruguay and Argentina. (Uruguay won 4–2.)

259. 1991; the USA won.

260. Three: 220 yard dash; 220 yard hurdles and the long jump. (He also equalled the record for the hundred yard dash.)

261. Iffley Road.

262. Five.

263. Thirteen days.

264. They were/are Formula One racing drivers.

265. Spartakiada.

266. 11 – they are numbers on a dartboard.

267. Tiddlywinks.

268. Jackie Rae.

269. Twice.

270. Sumo Wrestling.

271. Primo Carnera.

272. There isn't one. The course is owned by the local corporation and, as a municipal facility, players tee off on a first come, first served basis. (Severiano Ballesteros found this out to his chagrin in 1991 when, fancying a bit of practice, he turned up only to be refused admittance because Mr McGregor, a local undertaker, had taken the last available place for the day.)

273. Roller skates. (He certainly impressed the revellers at the party for whilst these first roller skates operated with great efficiency allowing him to enter the hall at speed, he had not bent his mind to the problems of turning or stopping. He crashed into a highly expensive glass panel breaking that, his nose, his right arm and the violin he was playing at the time.)

274. The yo-yo. (This was an ancient weapon also used for knocking monkeys out of trees.)

275. 1661. Charles II wagered one of his boats against that of the Duke of York in a race from Greenwich to Gravesend and back. (Previously yachts had been used mainly as pursuit craft by pirates, the boat's very name deriving from the German *jagen*, to hunt.)

276. 1807. (Allow five years either way.)

277. Bowls. It was considered harmful to manly development.

278. Folk dancing.

279. Ascot race-course.

280. Golf.

281. Queensberry Rules. (The Marquess of Queensberry had nothing to do with drawing them up, he simply sponsored Chambers's labours.)

282. The Jockey Club.

283. The first officiated cycle race.

284. They were allowed to play on Sundays.

285. Poker. As introduced by US ambassador Robert Cummings Schenck.

286. Mike Tyson.

287. Willie Shoemaker.

288. Cricket – Kent won.

289. The Derby, as organised by the 17th Earl of Derby.

290. The Marylebone Cricket Club (MCC).

291. Oslo.

292. Gary Kasparov.

293. The America's Cup.

294. The 1860s. (1862.)

295. 1863.

296. 142. (Allow fifteen either way.)

297. 1973 in Kingston, Jamaica.

298. France – July 1894, between Paris and Rouen. (Peugeot took the first prize.)

299. James Gordon Bennett (of exclamation fame).

300. Basketball. He quite literally cut the bottoms out of two wastepaper baskets and nailed them up at opposite ends of the gym.

301. Fencing.

302. Motor Racing.

303. Dennis Taylor.

304. Eight.

305. Scheduled to start 1942 but not actually held until 1951.

306. Sapporo

307. Boxing.

308. In the 17th century.

309. Twenty four. (Allow within five each way.)

310. Five feet. (Allow with a few inches either way.)

311. Between about 8¾ and 9¾ inches.

312. 140.

313. Fifteen, (with a margin of at least two points).

314. Cut-throat.

315. Fifteen.

316. Croquet.

317. No longer than 300 yards.

318. Twelve.

319. Two with an extra one dealt face up if requested.

320. Twenty – all cards lower than a seven are removed.

321. Twenty-eight.

322. White.

323. Seventeen tiles long (by two tiles high).

324. Craps or crap dice.

325. 121. (Incidentally, during the late 1960s the *News of the World* 'card corner' column had more requests for information on cribbage than on any other game.)

326. Between 6,500 and 7,000 yards long. (Allow within five hundred yards either way.)

327. Patrick.

328. Richard.

329. Twelve.

330. Martina Navratilova – she beat Monica Seles in the 1993 Paris Open competition.

331. Thirty-six.

332. Nothing. Debts incurred through gambling are not recoverable by English law – or by law in many parts of the world for that matter. (Interestingly this also means that your local casino owner couldn't make punters pay their debts either, hence their reported predilection for keeping large collection 'agents' on their payroll.)

333. Kublai Khan.

334. Persimmon.

335. The Derby, the St Leger and the Two Thousand Guineas.

336. Around 70 mph.

337. About a quarter of a mile.

338. Three metres.

339. Lausanne.

340. Three: 1916, 1940 and 1944.

341. About sixty-five. (Accept any answer within five either side.)

342. Swimming.

343. Seven.

344. Umiak. (It is an open vessel as opposed to the kayak which is enclosed, apart from a space for the occupant.)

345. Four: roller hockey, roller derby, artistic skating and speed skating.

346. The International Lawn Tennis Federation.

347. Hurling.

348. Gymnastics.

349. 15–17 inches. (Allow two inches either way.)

350. Water ski-ing.

351. A Trampoline – a name he based on the Spanish *trampolin*, a spring board.

352. Lawn Tennis.

353. Kentucky Derby.

354. Billy Jean King.

355. 1970.

356. A new-style baseball bat introduced in 1884 by J Frederick Hillerich who had previously earned a living as a woodturner making bowling pins.

357. The New York Giants are based at the Polo Grounds.

358. Ingemar Johansson.

359. Pele.

360. 1894.

361. The Tour De France.

362. 1906.

363. 1952.

364. Sugar Ray Robinson.

365. Under twelve.

366. Maria Bueno.

367. Snooker.

368. The UK's first female general manager of a league team – Annie Bassett.

369. They feared the effect it would have upon male spectators!

370. Jimmy Connors.

371. Golf.

372. A boxing match.

373. She turned out to be a man.

374. The last bare-knuckle boxing contest – or at least

the last legal one. (They slugged it out for forty-two rounds, at the end of which the contest was declared a draw and each went their separate ways with a purse of two hundred guineas.)

375. Manchester United in 1968.

376. 1924.

377. 'My Old Kentucky Home'.

378. 5 ounces.

379. Nijinsky.

380. Ken Norten

381. Two and a half.

382. Ski-ing.

383. Ibrox Park, home ground of Glasgow Rangers.

384. Hammer throwing.

385. Fritjof Nansen.

386. Baseball.

387. Muhammed Ali.

388. Golf.

389. Diane Leather.

390. Chris Brasher.

391. Max Schmelling.

392. Chris Evert.

393. Swan-upping.

394. Golf.

395. Turnberry.

396. Five hours.

397. No, not baseball or football, but ice hockey.

398. Yes, it was Australia, you should have had the confidence to stick to the obvious answer!

399. A mooring rope.

400. John McEnroe.

401. Dunfermline.

402. 1956.

403. '41'.

404. The Frying Pan.

405. Buster Crabbe, Herman Brix and Glenn Morris.

406. Shot-put and Javelin.

407. Eight.

408. Fencing.

409. World Match Play.

410. Bobby Locke.

411. He used pedal power to fly the *Gossamer Albatross*.

412. Alan Knott.

413. Sharron Davies.

414. Anthony Armstrong-Jones, later Lord Snowdon.

415. Australia's Rodney Marsh.

416. Ice Hockey.

417. Golf clubs.

418. Sidecar racing.

419. Two.

420. David Gower/Gower Peninsula.

421. A double eagle.

422. W G Grace.

423. A gimmie, as in 'give me (the point)'.

424. They both won the F A Cup in successive years.

425. They should freeze – a mite difficult in mid-throw!

426. A googly.

427. Mary Queen of Scots.

428. Chris Chataway.

429. Kent.

430. Two ounces.

431. Fifteen.

432. As a child she had been crippled by polio.

433. Twenty-five.

434. Both have won the English grand slam.

435. Table tennis.

436. None – they did not compete.

437. Lynn Davis.

438. Olga Korbut.

439. She was Jewish and the Nazis were hosting the party.

440. Samantha Foggo – Olympic swimmer.

441. The 800 metres.

442. 1984.

443. His autograph.

444. *The Telegraph.*

445. 776 BC.

446. Four.

447. Table tennis.

448. Ron Clark.

449. 1936 Berlin Olympics.

450. Twelve hundred yards.

451. Four years. (Although people use the term to describe the actual meetings, 'olympiad' actually denotes the span of four years between the years of the meetings.)

452. Six yards.

453. He took the part himself.

454. Peter Fleming.

455. Stock Car racing.

456. Courtney Jones.

457. Snooker.

458. 1500 metres (in 3.56 minutes).

459. The Harlem Globetrotters.

460. Bridge.

461. Twenty-five years.

462. Golf and tennis.

463. Oxford.

464. Silverstone, in 1950.

465. Nineteen.

466. Ken Barrington.

467. Heather McKay.

468. Bradford Park Avenue.

469. Tennis.

470. 1748. (Allow fifty years either way.)

471. Ole Olson.

472. Gloucestershire.

473. The Fairs Cup.
474. Bowls.
475. Outside right.
476. Spain.
477. Two.
478. Monza.
479. The Autumn Double.
480. Tommy Stack.
481. Ten feet.
482. Floyd Patterson.
483. Run the 200 metres.
484. A bandit.
485. Newmarket.
486. Walter Hagen.
487. Bob Lutz.
488. Motor Rallying.
489. South Africa.
490. Manchester United.
491. Ski-ing.
492. Nijinsky.
493. Johnny Weissmuller.

494. Softball.

495. A vault.

496. 1928.

497. In a broken bottle.

498. Rugby League.

499. Douglas Jardine.

500. Orienteering.

501. Two minutes.

502. Floyd Patterson.

503. Greece.

504. Babe Ruth.

505. Melbourne.

506. Judo.

507. The Milk Race.

508. The full- and half-Nelson of wrestling.

509. British Association of Ski-ing Instructors.

510. Ten. (Allow within two of this answer.)

511. One minute.

512. Forest Hills.

513. Eight seconds.

514. Spin bowling.

515. Arsenal.

516. All three have won Junior Wimbledon.

517. Kent.

518. Rowing, Henley.

519. Badminton.

520. Princess Anne, Goodwill was the name of the horse on which she competed.

521. Hickstead's All England jumping course.

522. It was to him that Harvey Smith made his famous gesture (a v-sign).

523. Moto-cross.

524. She was the first woman to referee a match between two male teams (1976).

525. Shooting.

526. Shergar was kidnapped.

527. John and Tracey Austin.

528. *Bolero*. (If we all had a pound for every time the end to that routine had been shown we would be pretty rich!)

529. Gary Sobers.

530. Twenty-nine times owing to bad weather (Allow an answer within five.)

531. The Grand Liverpool Steeplechase.

532. Naomi James. (She was also the first woman to sail solo round Cape Horn.)

533. Jennifer Capriati, in 1990, at the Virginia Slims tournament. (She was fourteen.)

534. The London Marathon – they had been neck and neck all the way and made the sporting gesture of holding each other's hand to cross the finishing line at the same time.

535. A badminton shuttlecock.

536. 1961.

537. London Welsh Rugby Club.

538. Seventeen.

539. John L Sullivan.

540. They all died in an air crash.

541. Prize fighter James Corbett.

542. Indonesia – badminton.

543. The nickname of a putter when used anywhere other than on the green.

544. The men's shot-weight.

545. Jersey Joe Walcott.

546. Jean Borotra, Rene Lacoste, Henri Cochet and Jacques Brunon.

547. Tokyo 1964.

548. Everyone competed naked – the very word *gymnasium* means to train whilst naked.

549. Jimmy Connors.

550. Billy Jean King.

551. Thirty-eight.

552. Table tennis.

PEOPLE, PLACES AND EVENTS

1. Susan B Anthony, (the American campaigner for women's rights).
2. It is the Spanish for fleet.
3. The Pyramids of Egypt; Hanging Gardens of Babylon; Statue of Zeus at Olympia; Temple of Artemis at Ephesus; Mausoleum of Halicarnassus; Colossus of Rhodes; Pharos (Lighthouse) of Alexandria.
4. Henry VI.
5. George II.
6. Fifteen, (since the 6th century).
7. The nickname was attached to him during the 16th century about two hundred years after his death.
8. London.

9. Forty-seven Czars are buried in the Kremlin.
10. Richard I, (the Lionheart).
11. Henry VI and Mary Stuart, Queen of Scotland.
12. Juneau in Alaska. It covers 3,108 square miles.
13. 570 miles. (Allow margin between 550 and 600.)
14. John Locke.
15. Karl Marx wrote it in a letter to Engels.
16. Cape Agulhas.
17. Two.
18. Hiram Ulysses Grant.
19. 1825.
20. In the fifth century.
21. During the 1880s. (1888.)
22. In Casco Bay, Maine, USA.
23. California, Alaska and Hawaii.
24. Leon Trotsky.
25. Robert Walpole.
26. It is astride the Peru-Bolivia Border. (Accept either country.)
27. Devon.

28. Albania.

29. Admiral Pierre de Villeneuve.

30. Transylvanian Alps.

31. It rises in Staffordshire and empties into the Humber Estuary.

32. Lake Volta.

33. 14th century. (Actually, 1301 so accept 13th or 14th.)

34. Berkshire.

35. Wall Street.

36. Leicestershire, Northamptonshire, Oxfordshire, Gloucestershire, Hereford and Worcester and West Midlands.

37. Woking.

38. South Yemen.

39. On the Ubangi River.

40. Plutonium waste.

41. The Christian church.

42. Ian Paisley – he shouted it during a speech given by the Pope at the European Parliament.

43. She was accused of murdering seven men and was alleged to be America's first female serial killer.

44. He landed his light aircraft in Red Square.

45. Fidel Castro.

46. Michael Dukakis.

47. Floods.

48. The assassination of John F Kennedy.

49. He was killed in an aircraft accident.

50. They were years when the General Election was not held on a Thursday.

51. Wimbledon.

52. American.

53. A Spyder.

54. Michael Jordan – basketball player.

55. They were all victims of Jack the Ripper.

56. They were all subjects on British commemorative stamps in 1994.

57. Seven.

58. Charles Stuart Parnell.

59. New Zealand.

60. A giant condom – it was to publicize World AIDS Day.

61. Helen Sharman.

62. £2 million.

63. The USSR – he had been orbiting in a Russian space station for many months, by the time he returned the USSR had finally broken up.

64. Lake Itasca.

65. Admiral.

66. University of The Third Age.

67. The Mozambique Channel.

68. The perfume was called Champagne – Champagne producers won the right to have the perfume renamed in France.

69. About three thousand years ago.

70. Alaska.

71. Albany.

72. Forty-one.

73. Alcoholics Anonymous.

74. Siberia. (Accept Russia.)

75. In the 1850s, as a response to the lessons learned in the Crimean War.

76. Aleutian Islands.

77. Henry VII.

78. Andorra.

79. Queen Anne.

80. She was a pirate.

81. Thirty-nine. (Accept any answer between thirty-five and forty.)

82. To encourage tree planting.

83. Armagh.

84. Arran.

85. American Indians.

86. Pharoah Khafre.

87. T S Eliot's.

88. The Cistercian order.

89. 92 metres below sea level. (Accept any answer between 75m and 100m.)

90. Mount Everest.

91. In 1833. All the duties that used to belong to the Exchequer are now performed by the treasury.

92. It was called *Bock's Car*.

93. Kokura.

94. Seven.

95. The Encyclopaedia Britannica.

96. Eleven: Pembroke; St Johns; New; Corpus Christi; Jesus; St Catherine's; Christ's College/Christ Church; Jesus; Magdalen/Magdalene; Queen's; St Edmunds. (Accept any answer from nine to thirteen.)

97. Pitcairn Island.

98. Stoke, Tunstall, Burslem, Hanley, Fenton and Longton.

99. Montgomery and Radnor (small parts along the southern border do connect to Mid-Glamorgan and Gwent – so allow those answers too).

100. Kent.

101. Rotorua.

102. S S *Great Britain* – designed by Isambard Kingdom Brunel.

103. Sir Winston Churchill. (The Duke of London was the suggested title.)

104. The repeal of the Red Flag Law; November 13 was the last day on which cars were restricted to four miles an hour.

105. Window Tax – it was first introduced in 1696.

106. Brighton Pavilion.

107. Eighty-nine years; from 1750 when they were

created by the author Henry Fielding until 1839 when they were officially disbanded.

108. Blue.

109. She did not become Electress of Hanover – the Hanoverian crown could not be inherited through the female line.

110. William IV, on November 14 1834.

111. She was the model for the picture of Britannia which has been used on British coinage throughout the last three centuries.

112. The Irish Parliament.

113. Buxton.

114. Milwaukee Depth. (30,238 feet/9,219 metres – about 5 miles deep.)

115. 1967.

116. Eleven centuries – circa 395 AD to 1500 AD. (Accept any answer between nine and thirteen centuries.)

117. Black Bartholomew.

118. Kansas and Arkansas.

119. The Netherlands was fighting for its independence from Spain.

120. Easter Island.

121. The American Civil War, which cut off practically all supplies of cotton to British manufacturers.

122. East central North Island, New Zealand.

123. Indiana; Illinois; Iowa; Missouri; Nevada; Kansas.

124. The Cordilleras. (From the Old Spanish *cordilla* – cord or little rope.)

125. 1942 (May 4–8).

126. The River Dane.

127. Diego.

128. German mercenaries under contract to the French crown.

129. An elk. (This unenviable set of gnashers were held apart by strong springs. So, once fitted, he had to keep his jaws clamped shut. His party trick involved the entertainment of his guests by releasing and reclamping at top speed whilst pushing in celery and carrots as if they were going in through a shredder – so now you know what they did before television!)

130. A job – he joined the banking house of Lazard Brothers.

131. Dunnet Head and Lizard Point.

132. The chain-mail safety curtain lowered in 19th century theatres in the event of fire to place a barrier between the auditorium and the stage.

133. The Grey House. In the American War of Independence it sustained severe fire damage and was painted white to cover up the black stains.

134. Louis XVI.

135. Florence Nightingale.

136. An owl.

137. The Turkish Army. It was a concertinaed tube of fire-proofed linen with a candle set in a metal tray at the bottom.

138. He kidnapped and murdered Charles Lindbergh's child.

139. Empty tomb.

140. Marengo – he was eventually brought to a British stud farm where he lived a long and happy life.

141. They have all served time in prison.

142. None of them was.

143. They all died falling off the toilet – not the same toilet. (There is a rumour that Catherine died engaged in bizarre antics with a horse – not true.)

144. Black. The average person was not overburdened with money and knew they could only afford one purpose-made dress. Black became popular so it could double up for mourning.

145. Charles Lindbergh – he was only the first to do

it solo and prove that he could stay awake for thirty-odd hours.

146. They were the only six people to be executed in the Tower of London – the normal place for executions was outside the Tower on Tower Hill.

147. Admiral William Penn, Penn's father. The son was a Quaker and that sect regards eponymous honour as the sin of pride.

148. Jamaica.

149. *Conqueror.*

150. They were the leaders of the 1916 Easter Rebellion.

151. Benjamin Disraeli.

152. *Carpathia.*

153. General Leopoldo Galtieri.

154. The SuperGun destined for Iraq.

155. Woodrow Wilson.

156. Lord Acton.

157. Jesse James.

158. *Exxon Valdez.*

159. Australian PM, Bob Hawke.

160. Two bombs were thrown at him in St Petersburg, the second one killed him.

161. The British pound note.

162. Herman Goering.

163. Twenty – it was the maximum penalty allowed for a person under the age of twenty on the day of his crime.

164. Paul McCartney.

165. 1925.

166. Gravesend in Kent. She died of smallpox during a visit to the English court.

167. Patagonia.

168. They were both five feet five inches tall.

169. 1815, (on January 9 if you want to be precise – the end of the 'War of 1812'.)

170. Twenty-six.

171. Theodore Roosevelt. (JFK was the youngest *elected* at forty-three, but Roosevelt was already serving as vice-president at the age of forty-two and assumed office after the assassination of McKinley in 1901.)

172. They were either hanged or crushed to death under heavy stones – no witches were ever burnt at the stake, a privilege reserved for heretics and those guilty of treason.

173. Party political 'whip' as named from the 'Whipper In',

the man responsible for keeping the pack bunched and in order when moving through towns etc.

174. In a cellar under the House of Lords, not the Commons.

175. New York – the Big Apple. In Spanish *manzana* means apple, but in Hispanic slang it means a large important building or any central complex.

176. They were pregnant.

177. Tokyo.

178. Hang Seng.

179. David Koresh.

180. Kim Campbell – the first woman Prime Minister of Canada.

181. It was dedicated to the honour of the 11,500 women who had served their country during the Vietnam War.

182. The Maastricht Treaty.

183. Less than 10%.

184. Saddam Hussein at the outbreak of the Gulf War.

185. They were banned under the 1991 Dangerous Dogs Bill.

186. Peter Wright.

187. His wife Nancy consulted an astrologer to find out which dates would be the most auspicious.

188. Amnesty International.

189. Argentina, Brazil and Chile.

190. Estonia.

191. President J F Kennedy.

192. Cory Aquino.

193. Emmeline Pankhurst.

194. 1932.

195. Queen Elizabeth I.

196. Las Vegas.

197. William Lamb, who later became the 2nd Viscount Melbourne. (Accept either name.)

198. The Caspian Sea.

199. *Ritter.*

200. Kingston-upon-Thames, Malden, Coombe and Surbiton.

201. Francis Bacon – he was appointed by Queen Elizabeth I as 'Queen's counsel extraordinary'.

202. Frankfort.

203. 1944. (Oct 24.)

204. July 1.

205. (Jude) Thaddeus.

206. Juan Carlos of Spain

207. Gold bullion. (The wreck had lain in the Barents Sea for about forty years after being sunk by German destroyers and U-boats. Her cargo was being transported from Russia to Britain. When the bullion was finally retrieved, 45% of its value went to the salvage company whilst the remainder was distributed between the Soviet and British governments.)

208. He was in Bolivia and was caught by Bolivian Army troops.

209. £2.1 billion. (Accept two or three billion.)

210. John Major, Michael Heseltine and Douglas Hurd.

211. November 1990.

212. Nicholas Ridley.

213. Charles Wilson.

214. Bhagwan Shree Rajneesh.

215. Nina Temple.

216. Ron Brown – he was MP for Edinburgh Leith.

217. Barbara Bush.

218. HMS *Brilliant*.

219. Edith Cresson.

220. Winnie Mandela, charged with kidnapping and assault.

221. Roger Cooper, a British businessman who had been held on charges of espionage.

222. Waterloo. (The thinking was sound. A good long bow outranged the musket by about two hundred yards – total range was killing range; unlike the musket, even an untrained man could put twenty arrows into the air and leave the rest to gravity in the time it took the opposition to load and fire a musket – it would have been the closest thing to a machine gun of the time. It was only the fear of looking stupid, if anything went wrong, by going up against French musketry with bows and arrows that prevented it.)

223. Ffyona Campbell.

224. Spain, at Bunyol in the south-eastern region.

225. Hong Kong. The Chinese army have declared that they will set up its headquarters there when the colony reverts to China in 1997.

226. Israel's.

227. Food critic Egon Ronay.

228. Richard Branson sued British Airways over their attempts to rid themselves of Branson's competition.

229. Lawrence.

230. Captain Robert Scott in his account of his South Polar expedition.

231. HMS *Hermes* and HMS *Invincible*.

232. Prince Michael of Kent.

233. Mairead Corrigan and Betty Williams.

234. Harold Wilson.

235. The Great Wall of China; The Terra-Cotta Army of Xian.

236. Lord Lucan.

237. Isabel.

238. Flixborough, Humberside.

239. Ten.

240. The Symbionese Liberation Army.

241. 1st Queen's Dragoon Guards.

242. Badminton Horse Trials.

243. William, (third and fourth names – Leonard Spencer).

244. Thursday.

245. Senator George McGovern.

246. 1972.

247. Reginald Maudling.

248. Idi Amin.

249. Ink. (The protest was actually nothing to do with the

EEC, it centred instead on the plans to redevelop Covent Garden.)

250. Stenay, France.

251. 18.

252. Five – Atlantic, Pacific, Indian, Arctic and Antarctic.

253. Reyjavik and Helsinki.

254. Chernobyl.

255. Every person in the village had voted for him – 100 per cent turn out!

256. Mali.

257. Paraguay and Bolivia.

258. Alaska.

259. 7,100. (Allow five hundred either way.)

260. The East India Company. (The rebelling locals locked up the British in their own dungeon – and they've been moaning about it ever since.)

261. Greenland.

262. It is an island off the coast of Massachusetts.

263. Lake Champlain.

264. The Spree.

265. The land parcels for Beverley Hills home development – the smartest council estate in the world! (Hence, of course, Rodeo Drive.)

266. The CIS, (former USSR.)

267. 25,000 miles – the earth is not a perfect sphere but oblate, thus from pole to pole it is 26.7 miles less.

268. Nuclear submarines.

269. Canada.

270. Sorry – it has the world's largest molybdenum mine.

271. China. Urumqui, regional capital of Hinjiang Uygur, is 2,500 miles from the sea.

272. Birmingham.

273. The Dead Sea.

274. 1500. (Allow within two hundred either way.)

275. New Guinea.

276. Wheat.

277. 75% of it. (Allow any reasonable approximation to this figure.)

278. North Dakota.

279. Both were established as religious enclaves.

280. Twelve.

281. La Paz in Bolivia.

282. Active volcanoes.

283. Iraq.

284. French, Italian, German, Romansche.

285. Brisbane.

286. Oranges. (But when did you last see an American orange? So what do they do with them all?)

287. Burkina Faso.

288. Richmond, Virginia.

289. South Shetland Islands in 1976.

290. Russia didn't own Alaska in the first place, they just convinced the Americans they did.

291. Bering Sea.

292. Japan.

293. Venezuela, because it reminded them of Venice.

294. Methadone.

295. Barbados.

296. Norway.

297. Laos.

298. Chile.

299. Yangon.

300. Guernsey.

301. Central Park.

302. Venezuela and Ecuador. (Venezuela was one of the founder members.)

303. Rome and Sheffield. (Incidentally, Rome was not named after Romulus who was a mythical character – the name actually derives from the ancient name of the Tiber, the Ruma or Roma which means 'to flow'.)

304. The Straits of Hormuz.

305. Greenland.

306. Bolivia.

307. Antarctica.

308. Ross Island – in the Ross Sea on the fringes of Antarctica.

309. 1949.

310. Brazil.

311. Netherlands. (The *Haarlems Dagblat.*)

312. The Amazon.

313. Niagara River.

314. Brazil.

315. The Vatican City.

316. Volgograd.

317. Colorado.

318. Madrid.

319. 220 miles. (Allow within twenty miles.)
320. 400. (Allow fifty either side.)
321. Mexico City.
322. Russia and her satellite countries.
323. Berchtesgaden.
324. Marseilles.
325. Big Ben. (This is the chiming bell not the clock or tower. Hall was commissioner of works for London at the time of casting.)
326. Bougainville.
327. Only two, Ecuador and Chile.
328. The USA.
329. New Orleans.
330. 75%.
331. Joan of Arc and Charles VII – Dauphin or King of France.
332. Vienna.
333. Paraguay.
334. Japan.
335. Montana, USA.
336. Macedonia, of the former Yugoslavia.
337. Quebec.

338. Kathmandu.

339. Spain.

340. Twenty to one.

341. Birmingham, Alabama.

342. Amazon.

343. Two; Spanish and Quechua.

344. The Aleutian Islands.

345. Leonid Brezhnev.

346. US.

347. Los Angeles.

348. Brazil.

349. 128. (Allow twenty either side. Each step is a regulation 33 inches giving an overall speed of four miles per hour.)

350. None. (This was nothing more than Lincoln playing to the gallery – he issued a bill telling the South to release all its slaves and the South declined and carried on as normal. An illustrative parallel would be for Britain to issue a bill demanding that China release all its political prisoners.)

351. Stonehenge – it was sold at auction along with its surrounding fields.

352. September 1981.

353. The Shah of Iran.

354. Elizabeth Ann Bayley Seton.

355. She was a photo-journalist.

356. Her daughter, Juliana.

357. Yugoslavia.

358. Fifty years.

359. Brighton beach.

360. Port of Spain's television station.

361. Arthur Phillip Louis.

362. 1990. (Two women deacons were ordained in St Anne's Cathedral, Belfast as the Church of Ireland gave women equal opportunity with men in that year.)

363. Surrender of Argentinian forces in the Falklands.

364. John Paul Getty II.

365. Juno, Sword, Gold, Omaha, Utah.

366. Giovanni Giacomo.

367. S S *Hampshire*.

368. About six months. (Abdication December 10 1936 – marriage June 3 1937.)

369. The British driving test.

370. Adolf Eichmann.

371. Elton John.

372. Two; Anne of Cleves (number four) and Catherine Parr (number six).

373. He used the verse 'If a man takes his brother's wife, it is impurity . . .' to argue that the marriage to Catherine of Aragon should never have taken place as it was against God's law. He won, of course.

374. Norman Shelley was an actor who recorded three of Winston Churchill's most famous speeches for broadcast during the 1940s. Until the 1990s the public had always assumed the words were spoken by Churchill himself.

375. Bianca.

376. Mussolini's mistress.

377. He was shot. (Do not accept hanging – he was hung from the lamp-post after his death.)

378. Carmel. He was elected on April 8 1986.

379. Hollywood's abuse of American Indians.

380. 1991. Its dismantling was part of the INF disarmament treaty.

381. In the 1880s.

382. 1990 – February 11.

383. Greenland.

384. November 1941 – when Mongolian cavalry charged

German infantry outside Moscow. Two and a half thousand of that cavalry were killed against zero casualties for the Germans.

385. Infantry – from the Latin *infans*. (Whilst this is obvious in words such as infant, foot-soldiers were originally those on the battlefield without a banner to 'speak' their name to the enemy, unlike the knights who announced themselves with heraldic device and family flag.)

386. NCO's chevrons on the sleeves – representative of a lance broken in combat. There is, of course, also the rank of Lance Corporal.

387. Brigadier – he who once led the brigands.

388. Torquemada – as in 'torque', to twist.

389. Caligula – the Latin for 'little boots'.

390. Maxwell House coffee.

391. The wearing of the tartan.

392. Prairie Schooners. (Conestoga also produced a distinctive, tapered cigar. First known as a conestoga this later shortened to stogie – a term later shifting to any cigar.)

393. The Devil's Advocate.

394. The Sahara.

395. The Burning Bush. Popularly known in that neck of the woods as the gasplant, the shrub gives off a

highly volatile vapour causing the bush, in summer, to erupt suddenly in a sheet of flame. The eruption is so sudden and violent that the host-plant usually remains unscarred by the event.

396. Berwick-on-Tweed. So close to the Scottish border it used to have to be named as being in or out; and that noble town was included in the sport with 'The Bear', better known as the Crimean War, the Russians finally and formally acknowledging peace with Berwick in 1965.

397. 1871.

398. Lancaster is red; York is white.

399. Rodrigo Borgia – boy, did he die with a surprised look on his face!

400. 150 years ago. It was totally unknown to the Hebrew people at the time of King David and is in fact an ancient Hindu symbol.

401. They were all one-time circus wire acts.

402. France.

403. Friday.

404. Albania.

405. Martinique – she was a Creole.

406. George III who was completely mad was on the throne so no one could put on a play about a batty monarch.

407. Of Winston Churchill when he lost the Manchester seat.

408. Sixty-four.

409. The three cornered hat or tricorn.

410. Wallis Simpson was introduced to the Prince of Wales.

411. A polar bear.

412. The top hat. He attraced such a crowd that a young woman was jostled into the path of a passing hansom cab and run over. He was fined five guineas for 'wearing upon his head a tall structure of shining lustre calculated to disturb persons of timid disposition'.

413. 'Greensleeves'.

414. Mary, Queen of Scots.

415. The first general post office.

416. It was announced on that day that in 1993 Poll Tax would be replaced by the new Council Tax.

417. The dismantling of the Berlin Wall.

418. 1990.

419. Perestroika, announced by Gorbachev.

420. Jonathan Wild. (The gallows of Tyburn stood to the west of the old city of London, on a site corresponding to modern Marble Arch; the expression 'gone west' was coined by the London criminal

fraternity to explain the absence of one of their chums who had gone for a spin in the municipal tumbril.)

421. 1741.

422. Iran released fifty-two American hostages after 444 days of detention.

423. London and Bristol.

424. The independence of India.

425. Fortnum and Mason's, the former being the royal flunkey.

426. Two years hard labour.

427. The Salvation Army.

428. Florence Nightingale and her nurses.

429. Manchester.

430. Cleopatra and Mark Antony.

431. Helen Keller.

432. Buffalo Bill's.

433. Butter – he wanted something which didn't go off so quickly and margarine was the answer.

434. Pentateuch.

435. 102. (Allow within twenty either way. They were notably unpopular with the sailors in the crew who resented being told not to swear, spit, drink and

smoke. They apparently called their precious cargo the Puke Stockings which did not much improve harmony on board.)

436. German.

437. William III.

438. Napoleon.

439. Winston.

440. On Mars.

441. Richard I (Lionheart).

442. Thomas More, canonised in 1920.

443. Peter the Great.

444. Cannibalism. Packer had been hired as a guide by a group of prospectors whom he led into an early winter. Holed up in a shack, Packer realised the only decent food he was likely to see before spring was stamping round the cabin bitching about his lousy organisation. Packer was tried before Judge Edwin Cade who, a staunch Democrat nominee, uttered the immortal line: 'Packer, you are a lowdown, depraved son-of-a-bitch – there are only twelve democrat voters in the whole of Hinsdale County and you ate seven of them'.

445. Toby.

446. Debtors.

447. To ride up and down the new-fangled escalators all

day to prove to the more timid members of the public that if he, Harris, with a wooden leg was safe then anyone would be.

448. Twenty miles per hour.

449. The Magi. (Accept the Three Kings or Three Wise Men.)

450. Maurice.

451. Queen Victoria.

452. Hubert Humphrey.

453. George V.

454. Colonel Henry Shrapnel.

455. London, Durham, Kent, York, Lancaster.

456. It is regarded as the centre of England.

457. Sir William Harcourt.

458. 1946.

459. Slaves.

460. The White Star Line.

461. They are a voluntary group formed in the US who act as a protection force for citizens on the underground etc. They now have off-shoots throughout the world.

462. 1952.

463. Smokeless Zone.

464. The surname of Windsor.

465. 1978 in Oldham.

466. 1989.

467. 1966.

468. Sir Francis Chichester.

469. Robert Kennedy.

470. WPC Yvonne Fletcher.

471. Louis Mountbatten.

472. The Battle of Waterloo – he was the Duke of Wellington.

473. 1918.

474. James Earl Ray.

475. The Channel Tunnel project.

476. The Bay of Pigs fiasco in Cuba.

477. Olaf Palme.

478. 1947.

479. With a huge party to mark the completion of a massive re-furbishment and clean-up.

480. 1972.

481. Harold Wilson and Ian Smith.

482. Shah of Iran – Reza Pahlavi.

483. Black Monday. Fifty billion pounds were wiped from share values during the course of the day's trading on the Stock Exchange.

484. She was accused of employing illegal aliens and failing to pay the necessary Social Security payments for them.

485. The last sea battle fought between galleys.

486. Bamboo.

487. Genghis Khan. (4.9 million square miles which he held and controlled for nearly twenty-two years.)

488. Dick Whittington. (Yes, there really was such a chap – three times Mayor of London.)

489. Because Charles I sold them to raise money for the civil war – Cromwell and his gang got rid of the rest of the royal treasures by selling them off.

490. Thermopylae – the first part obviously means hot and the second means 'gate' and is also responsible for the electrical pylon, the lower part of which looks like an ancient gate.

491. Tea, which was otherwise subject to a very high import tax.

492. The Pyrenees and the Alps.

493. They were all pronounced stutterers.

494. François I and our own Henry VIII who lost.

495. Three.

496. 1929.

497. Curfew. This was not a policing matter but intended for domestic safety. (The term derives from the French *couvre feu* basically meaning to cover the fire and called for all fires to be extinguished, as William was fed up with all the wooden buildings burning down.)

498. Nineteen years. From 1568 to 1587.

499. Cervantes. (Incidentally, he died on exactly the same date as Shakespeare.)

500. English – previously much of the business was conducted in Latin or French.

501. Italy – it was the Romans.

502. Trotsky, in Mexico City.

503. Because he was a Japanese soldier who didn't know that the Second World War had finished.

504. A bear, because he was told he couldn't keep dogs in the room.

505. Because he was illiterate.

506. Nine.

507. Carry Nation, temperance campaigner.

508. Robert de Bruis – whose name became corrupted to Robert the Bruce.

509. The Order of Merit.

510. The religious council believed that their oscillating motion was responsible for the prevailing drought. Unfortunately for sanity and logical thought, it absolutely chucked it down the day after the ban!

511. The *Bismarck* battleship.

512. Adams.

513. Richard Nixon.

514. Metal from Russian guns captured at Sebastapol in the Crimean War.

515. Edward II.

516. In prison in Genoa.

517. The Antonine Wall.

518. Further south than Lancashire or Yorkshire at St Albans.

519. Thomas Jefferson.

520. Returning Crusaders.

521. 1975.

522. Admiral Charles Howard.

523. Queen Christina of Sweden.

524. A wedding ring, hence that city being otherwise known as the Bride of the Sea.

525. Warfield.

526. Louis Mountbatten.

527. They were chopped up, boiled and the bits shoved into honey jars. (Worth going abroad for, wasn't it?)

528. His arm.

529. To visit the shrine of Thomas à Becket.

530. Napoleon – that was his favourite flower.

531. The Korean War.

532. They were capturing the Hubble telescope to make repairs. To do this they made a record five space walks.

533. Roman Catholicism.

534. Edgar Allan Poe.

535. James I.

536. Wild Bill Hickok.

537. Eton. (New Zealander John Lewis.)

538. Eaglesham, near Glasgow.

539. Eurodisney.

540. Buckingham Palace.

541. Foreign currency.

542. Stella Rimington.

543. General Charles de Gaulle.

544. Milford Haven.

545. An initiative whereby toy retailers gave $100 toy vouchers for every gun handed in.

546. Boutros Boutros Gali.

547. *Observer.*

548. The 14th century covered wooden bridge.

549. His brother, Prince Albert.

550. The release of Ivan Demjanjuk, accused of being a death camp guard, after an extradition and trial process lasting eight years.